A COLLECTION OF ESSAYS

MORMON WOMEN SPEAK

EDITED BY MARY LYTHGOE BRADFORD

Olympus Publishing Company, Salt Lake City, Utah

Printed in the United States of America
First Printing December 1982

Designed by: Kathy Lee

Library of Congress Catalog Card Number: 82-62366
ISBN: 0-913420-94-8

Contents

Preface

I collect friendships with women, especially Mormon women who have enriched my life with their advice, their laughter, their confessions, their dreams and disappointments, their sorrows—most of all with their faith. It is fitting that one of those friendships should lead to this book.

Marion Mangum came to me with an idea for a book of personal essays to be written by Mormon women. Would I edit such a book? At first I said no. I was deep into the planning of *Dialogue's* tenth anniversary women's issue and so wouldn't have time for anything else. Then it occurred to me that the two projects could be joined. Since the Silver Foundation had offered to fund a writing contest for the journal, the winners of the contest and some of the entries could form a book. Our announcement brought immediate response from a host of writers. The results remind me of many good gatherings of Mormon women—warm, thoughtful, often humorous, sometimes tearful—but always a generous sharing of the difficulties and the joys of life in Mormon country.

A very few of our contributors are professional writers; a few have published before, but most are sandwiching writing chores between back-breaking responsibilities at home, church and community. They have all chosen to express themselves in one of the most deceptively difficult of all forms, one just coming into its own in Mormon letters. Not a diary entry, not a true confession, not really an autobiography nor a sermon, the personal essay shares the traits of all of these but is more demanding. Some of the entries in our contest told interesting, gripping stories but were not organized to a specific purpose; others were well-organized and eloquent but so sermonizing in tone that the important personal touch was lost. Some of those willing and able to learn the craft of the essay and to stay through a sometimes arduous editing process are presented here. As their editor, I thank them for their generosity. They have welcomed me into their inner rooms for gratifying glimpses of lives well-lived. I am humbled by their courage, their realism and their idealism. I hope though, that this book is only a beginning. To all of those who did not make it into this collection for one reason or another, I say, try again! We have only begun to write!

I am also grateful to friends and colleagues who contributed valuable listening, copy editing and typing services; Annette Sorensen Rogers, Sandy Ballif Straubbahr, Lorraine Bradford, and especially, Julie Randall.

Mary Lythgoe Bradford

Arlington, Va.
November 1, 1982

Mary L. Bradford

Introduction

"Writing helps me figure things out," says Dian Saderup, one of the essayists in this book. The other twenty-three also have used writing to sort out the events and the philosophies of their lives. They have chosen to risk themselves in writing, as makers and doers with the courage to embody their faith in words. "A saint is someone who is taking a risk," Dian goes on: "Living is doing, doing means choosing and choosing means taking risks." It is not easy for women who have been taught to practice self-effacement, modesty, and service to others suddenly to come out into the light of the personal essay. These writers had to be willing to face their own ambivalence, guilt, unrealized dreams and failures. But their willingness to do so gave them the courage to embark on a quest, a journey, an adventure on the road to wholeness and healing.

This quest is illustrated on our cover by the graphic symbol of the mandala. In Jungian terms, this means "the self, the wholeness of the personality which if all goes well is harmonious, but which cannot tolerate self-deception."[1] An image that extends back through primitive and not so primitive cultures—Chinese, Indian, American Indian,[2] it is present today in art, religion and psychology. Drawn as a circle or a sphere and usually divided into four parts around a center and held together by a protective circle, the mandala has a healing quality that invokes all the experiences of a lifetime. We have chosen to depict four aspects of the Mormon woman's life with a woman's face in the center. Through her home, her church, her service to others and the development of her own talents, this woman creates her mandala. Believing with Jung that the "Bettering of the general ill begins with the individual,"[3] she accepts responsibility for her own happiness, at the same time refusing to turn from the needs of others.

The writers in this collection are women engaged in the process of inner growth that leads to maturity. They work through the process by honestly looking at their own imperfections, sins and griefs. They refuse to let anger turn inward toward depression or outward toward destruction. Though struggling to develop talents in a confusing world, they juggle demanding roles in church and family, finding that "real liberation comes not from glossing over and repressing painful states of feelings, but only from experiencing them to the full."[4] In the words of Cherie Pedersen, "the multi-faceted nature of my own womanhood has given me the incentive to narrow the gap between what I am and what I wish to become."

Writing not only helps women figure things out, but it also helps to heal rifts and splits. Helen Stark recognizes dark places in herself which she calls the "witch" and decides that "if healing is to begin, I must befriend my alienated self . . . I must honor the creative potential within my own witch." Mary Ellen Romney MacArthur describes the split in her life when she left home to attend college a few miles away. She calls it "The Paso Robles Rift" for that midway point in the journey when she seemingly shed her home-church self for her college-educated self. Rubina Forester's experience with discrimination has led her to recognize a similar division within herself: "My educated self with the wider vision, the fuller understanding, the higher dream pits itself against the Polynesian half with its quicker generosity, its plainer faith, its simpler needs."

All of the women must come to terms with role expectations at home and at church. Ann Edwards-Cannon, recalls how she and her friends felt frustration in planning for the future and "our difficulty in reconciling our interests and the economic realities of today with what we (perhaps mistakenly) perceived as the traditional role of women in the church." Jerrie Hurd in making the decision to return to college recalls that she "half believed that success could be bought only by failure in the home and unwilling to fail at home, I didn't really expect to succeed in the world." Marlene Payne, however, recounts that early in life she knew that she would be able to have both home and career by deciding to "reconstruct the gospel anew" . . . in a pattern "consistent with my nature." And Jean Johnson, entering the workforce out of necessity, discovers that society gives "seeming rewards of love and protection for the woman who remains in some respects a child-like, semi-adult."

The search for self within the bonds of motherhood take poignant forms. Myrna Marler admits that "Motherhood did not come naturally to me" . . . while jubilant Elinor Hyde reminds us that "these are God's children, lent to you for a few short years. You are going to give it all you've got." And Gladys Clark Farmer decides that she will come to know herself only after she has learned to understand her own mother: "For what I am is not only a product of an era of 'liberated women'; it is also the result of and a reaction to the example of my own mother."

All of the essays raise quintessential questions about life

from birth to death and way stations between. The three prize-winning essays, (Judith Dushku, Maureen Beecher, Edna Laney) all deal with birth and death in the confines of family, church, community. Though none of the writers has arrived at her destination, all have reached insights worth sharing, and most are enjoying the journey. Elizabeth Wach, a humorous fictional essay, has St. Peter ask the obsessive-compulsive heroine "Did you have a good time?" This seemingly light question causes us to wonder about the endless goings and comings of our days, and leads us to the reconciliation of Loretta Randall Sharp who decides that "the Church does not exist in the abstract" and that "members constitute the Church, but the Savior cannot claim us until we function as a unified whole community single to the glory of God." And then in a fitting climax to this chorus of individual voices, she reminds us that the community of God is not one of "clones": "If we allow ourselves instruction from heavenly beings in different ways, and if we celebrate rather than fear differences in one another, we will do as our Heavenly Father commands: We will become one. We will receive the Holy Ghost."

The common themes in the lives of women combined with their exciting differences will ultimately lead them to create healing mandalas of their own lives—at peace with God, themselves and others.

---

[1]*Memories, Dreams, Reflections* by C.G. Jung, recorded and edited by Aniela Jaffe', trans. Richard and Clara Winston (New York: Pantheon Books, 1963). pp. 195ff..

[2]"A Study in the Process of Individuation," *Mandala Symbolism* by C.G. Jung, Bollinger Foundation (Princeton, N.J., Princeton University Press, 1969). p. 65.

[3]*Ibid.* p. 51.

"Writing helps me figure things out."
Dian Saderup

Dian Saderup

The Wall

"That's what we're put on this earth to do: to endeavor in the face of the impossible."—Margaret Drabble

I had back surgery last August. Now I have to stay inside my apartment until February while three of my vertebra fuse. The first month inside I spent almost all my time reading fat novels and escaping from my panic. Real claustrophobia. But now I'm more used to it. I can see, at least sometimes, what a peculiar luxury this six months is: the time after midnight when I can lie in my bed—not worried about sleep because it doesn't matter when I get up —and stare at the shadows made by the moonlight through the window; music to listen to—not music to do housework to or embroider to—but just listen to, me and Smetana and Beethoven, the Beatles or Willie Nelson. It's a thinking time, a time to sort out some of my experiences and try to understand a little of what it all means.

Writing helps me figure things out.

People suffer. That is a terrifying reality to me; not so much because I've suffered but because people I love have, people I don't know, people with flesh and bone and fears like my own. During this past year several events have brought this home to me. In February an eighteen-year-old friend of my sister's died of leukemia. She had lost her thick waist-length black hair in chemotherapy. Last April I had lunch with a friend of my brother's who had been in and out of psychiatric wards for seven years since spending three months in prison for dealing drugs. About that same time I became friends with a girl who had suffered mild retardation from birth. She's twenty-five and "wants a boyfriend like other girls—oh, I want that!" She curls her hair every morning, wears Chantilly cologne, and attends ward young adult activities. Recently, I watched Playing for Time on television, a film about prisoners at Auschwitz who formed an orchestra to perform for their captors, buying time with music. One of the women officers—so hard with the female inmates—paradoxically and unofficially adopted a small Jewish child. I cannot forget her haunting eyes the day the child was taken from her.

I don't understand it at all sometimes. When I think too much, I heap all the pains I know one on top of the other until they become a great dark wall in my mind; a wall that condemns me for the good things in my own life; a wall that tempts me almost irresistibly to throw away my belief in a loving and powerful God, or worse, turn from him in anger. In these past few months that feel so much like a state of suspended animation, I've approached the wall in a quieter—less frightened, less furious—frame of mind. I've built it up, then touched it, pressed my hands and head against it; tried to find how I and others might climb over, or bring it down, or perhaps transform it.

A number of years ago my dad was involved in a large-scale business project with a close friend of his. He put in heavy hours of thought, work, and travel to make the endeavor "go," knowing that success would mean long-hoped-for freedom from serious financial concerns. At the turning point toward fulfillment his friend turned too, cheating him of a great deal of money. My dad just sorted out the pieces of our finances and started at the beginning. When I was younger, he used to read to me from the New Testament on Sunday afternoons. I remember the many times he read, "Whosoever shall smite thee on thy right cheek, turn to him the other also . . . Love your enemies, bless them that curse you, pray for them which despitefully use you." When I asked my father why he didn't take legal action against his friend, all he said was, "It doesn't seem appropriate to me."

Vanessa Redgrave (whose politics I may not concur with, but whose acting is wonderful) once said, "Conviction is everything." While I don't agree that it is *everything,* I do feel it is a great deal. My dad is one of the people who've taught me that I am responsible to what I believe, and equally, important, for just what it is I choose to believe. I talked with a forty-six-year-old woman in my ward whose surgeon, when removing a benign tumor from her brain, had accidentally nicked a small artery which led to permanent paralysis of her left side. The old anger rose in me, the wall went up. When she needed genuine empathy and a hand toward courage, I gave her pity, all the while wondering how *anyone* could be called responsible for things they did or felt in this world so marked by random violence and precarious joys. I was chastened when two weeks later she called to ask if I would help her cut and sew an infant's gown for her first grandchild's blessing. At one point she wept in frustration as we worked on the tiny dress, apologizing repeatedly for her tears.

I want to better understand the workings of my own *conscience,* for this responsible attitude of others, despite sometimes impossible adversity, seems to be grounded in deepest conviction and yearning. It is an attitude I would like to have. A good friend who left the security of the Wasatch front last summer for a life on her own in New York City (quite a leap!) wrote to me several months after she'd moved:

> It seems to me that the biggest questions in life are questions of loyalties; to whom or to what am I going to give myself? I expressed that to this actor guy I went out with, and he didn't understand at all. He just wants to have as many good times as he can and do whatever he has to do to keep from getting "wrecked up." After I got home I thought, "Hey, you may not believe in loyalties but you've got them, buddy; they're just all to yourself."

I think she's right about the "actor guy" as well as about the biggest questions.

Everywhere around and within me is the crazy *multi*verse we live in—time, being, matter, and space all intertwined in an infinitude of diversity. Like God, I am a maker and a creator (granted, on a somewhat smaller scale), whether for good or ill. I affect however slightly the ever-unfolding shape of reality. Living is doing, doing means choosing, and choosing means taking risks. I have so many conflicting impulses: intellectually, spiritually, socially, creatively. What will a future portrait of *this* artist as a young woman look like? A spinster in wool jumpers and knee socks, a copy of D. H. Lawrence in one hand, the Articles of Faith in the other? A rosy Relief Society wife with three children in tow and a '77 Ford station wagon parked in the lot outside? A relic from the sixties who still flips peace signs at policemen and hums Lennon and McCartney tunes while waiting for the bus? I believe God would have me penetrate my countless tangled images of self but that he does not *shout* direction or inspiration at me. He knows I need to learn to hear *inwardly*.

It is interesting to me that Christ did not say "*Know* and be baptized and you shall be saved" but rather, "Believe and be baptized. . . ." The word *believe* seems underrated among many LDS people who prefer the more securely emphatic *know*, perhaps because belief doesn't offer a guarantee but only a vision of possibilities. Six years ago, as I was studying the restored Gospel, this was a stumbling block to me. I had read the Book of Mormon; I had fasted, attended Church, and tried to align my life with the teachings of Christ. I had even replaced my torn Levis and Mexican blouses for more conservative clothes, but I could not say I *knew*. There were still doubts; there was still my wall. Looking back on that time, I can see the process I was involved in (and continue to be involved in)—that of learning to perceive and trust the deepest impulses of my own spirit as it is quickened by the Lord's; of coming to touch and respond with free feeling and positive action to the finest fabric of my own soul. I was (and am) discovering my conscience.

I had felt God's voice on many occasions, for example, during my patriarchal blessing. It was five days after Christmas. I was between terms at Utah State, staying for a time alone. I didn't know the patriarch; and I felt strange as I entered his cinderblock cubicle. But the feeling, when he put his hands on my head, was light through my body. Afterwards, I embraced him spontaneously. We stood there for several moments, our arms tightly around one another. Then I left. I cannot deny the feelings I had had at that time and at other times. It was a matter of following where those feelings led, of trusting them despite my doubts, for I had both doubt and irrepressible belief. I still do.

Not long ago my older brother, who has been estranged from the Church for many years, asked me, "What's a saint? What does 'saint' mean?"

I thought for a careful moment: "A saint is someone who is taking a risk—"

My older brother (also inactive) interrupted: "Wrong. You've got it wrong; it's just the opposite, if anything."

I continued, "No, listen to me. A saint is taking the biggest risk anyone can take—the risk of a *lifetime.* He's saying, 'I believe Christ is who he says he is and that what he says about the meaning of life is true. I'm willing to trust the whisperings in myself that tell me this, to translate those delicate convictions into the million actions that make up *my life.*"

The wall has become the greatest challenge to my perception and development of the fragile, God-inspired intimations of my soul: it is big, dark, loud, angry, and insistent that whatever I do must ultimately be without meaning. And perhaps in a strange way this is a blessing: to see within and beyond it requires the most profound sensitivity I'm capable of. It requires enormous trust in the subtlest voices within me. It requires that I seek out (with the greatest care) my own conscience and that I accept the responsibilities that accompany it. Maybe in some far-off millennial day I will at last be so finely tuned that the slightest breath of God will stir me to response, like a carefully-constructed violin which, in the hands of a skilled musician, answers each flutter of finger, each nuance of touch.

The things that are beautiful to me, the things I love, are realities that color and invigorate my life. My friend

Sibyl's hair—that wild mass of red that spits gold in the sunlight—is as real as these six months of confinement. My father's broad hands, the ridiculous Russian hat he wears in cold weather, the pair of old temple garments he has wrapped around his prized first edition copy of the Book of Mormon in his dresser drawer, are all there along with my worry for his burden of extended family, business, and church responsibilities. The Wasatch mountains outside my eleventh story window have now finished their bright autumn brag and today the swollen grey clouds of December press up against them; everything is grey, white, silver-purple. I can see the brooding of winter, and my heart—so tight and anxious lately with decisions about schooling and marriage, general direction, starts with sudden feeling, like the dark flock of sparrows exploding into the air from the limbs of a barren tree.

I am grateful to God for beautiful things: for my mother playing "Bumble Boogie" or Beethoven's "Sonata Pathetique" on her fine piano; for the way my twenty-six-year old brother is always *jumping*—when he walks or plays in his rock band—like something electric, and for the things he didn't have to say when we heard that John Lennon had been killed; for my sister's Nastassia-Kinsky lips, almond eyes and flawless porcelain skin (when my own self-confidence is low, I sometimes feel a little like the negative alongside a perfectly developed photograph); for President Kimball's whisper voice as he rejoices with the Church at conference during the "sus . . .su . . . susk . . . susquicentennial." I could go on for pages because these are the things that are good, that say *yes, yes, yes.* They are as real as pain—indeed, sometimes take their richest substance from pain itself. They are as real as fear and uncertainty, as anger at injustice. They are to me as

"Julia's Clothes" must have been to the poet Robert Herrick: "Whenas in silks my Julia goes/ Then, then methinks how sweetly flows/ The liquification of her clothes./ Next when I cast mine eyes and see/ That brave vibration each way free/ Oh how that glittering taketh me." They are the shapes my loves are clothed with, and each in its own way is a glittering that takes me, that arrests my senses. Love is a kaleidoscope of pain and joy and everything in between. It is the best life gives me.

Gladys Clark Farmer

In Her Image

My nine-year-old daughter recently asked me a perceptive question: ''Mom, this year you're a PTA president; when I was little you were writing a book; what are you going to be doing next?''

''Anything but housework,'' I answered facetiously. I could tell that she was beginning to understand her mother—a woman with a variety of talents and interests and a compulsion to do things well. But she cannot really understand me until she also understands her 79-year-old grandmother who lives next door. For what I am is not only a product of an era of ''liberated women,'' it is also a result of and a reaction to the example of my own mother.

My mother, crippled with arthritis and osteoporosis, spends most of the day sitting in a soft chair with hot water bottles tucked around her. But she has not given up! Twice in the last three years she has faced surgery because of broken hips; twice she has been given little chance to live. Twice she has fought back and learned to walk again, slowly, painfully with the support of a walker. This has been difficult for me to watch because it contrasts so vividly with my childhood memories of her feet moving faster than most men's and her hands going non-stop.

The pace of her hands and feet represented the pace of her life. At the age of thirty-one, she had experienced a childhood in rural Illinois, a move to Utah, days of strenuous fruit picking (to earn money for school), graduation from BYU with a "normal" degree, three years of grade-school teaching, several years of nurses training, and years of teaching and supervising nurses in the Salt Lake LDS Hospital.

The greatest change of her life followed an invitation for dinner at the home of one of her nursing students. The other dinner guest was the student's brother, a forty-three-year-old rancher, school teacher, and widower with two young sons. My future father, immediately attracted to her, began a regular correspondence. She was impressed by his many fine qualities but hesitated sixteen months before she could bear to leave the life of a professional nurse she had learned to love.

After marriage in the Salt Lake Temple they set out on a honeymoon to Washington, D.C., New York City, and the Chicago World's Fair, a trip she described in her diary with enthusiasm and wonder. Twenty-six days later they arrived at a ranch in southeastern Idaho, a day she recorded thus: "I descended from a dream cloud to find butter to churn, bread to bake, a house to keep clean, family wash to do, and dinner meals to prepare for hay men." The honeymoon was indeed over. For the next thirty-seven years she lived and worked in that farm house, raising the two children as her own and giving birth to five more. She nursed babies while standing at the cooking stove, with so little time for personal care that she once endured an eight-day stretch without even stopping to comb her hair.

Her work was not only time-consuming but arduous. Washing meant pulling heavy cotton sheets and work overalls from an old tub washer; ironing meant pressing shirts with a heavy flat-iron heated on the wood stove; eating meant plucking, cleaning and canning chickens, raising and canning fruits and vegetables, baking bread, and churning butter. All summer, every summer she cooked for the hay crew that included not only her husband and six sons but eight hired men as well. These are typical entries from her diary: "Churned 7½ pounds of butter"; "Made 6 batches of soap"; "Took 20 dressed hens to Preston, Idaho"; "Put up 99 quarts of fruit." This level of activity continued day after day, year after year.

But there was order in her life. Each day had its assigned task. Monday—washing; Tuesday—ironing; Wednesday—bread making; Thursday—churning butter; Friday—cleaning house; Saturday—baking. When my father came from the garden above town with unexpected bushels of vegetables, the afternoon and evening were spent in unplanned canning. Yes, each season had its expected labors: summer and fall, canning food and feeding hay men; winter and spring, sewing, quilting, and housecleaning. I think the stability of her role helped make the demands bearable.

Because Church leaders in that era did not give heavy assignments to mothers with young children, the only call upon her time was homemaking. She held no church jobs during the years when we were small and once let two years pass without even attempting to dress for Church. The few civic responsibilities in the community of five hundred were assumed by the men of the village. Her only service outside the home was care of the sick people who needed immediate medical attention. That service she gave without hesitation and with much joy.

She never chauffeured any of her children to music,

swimming, or gymnastic lessons or to little league and soccer games. In fact, I have only one memory of her ever driving the car. As for entertaining children, I doubt that the thought crossed her mind. She expected us children either to help with the work or get out of the way and entertain ourselves. I can't recall ever playing a game with my mother, reading a book with her, or practicing the piano while she listened. Our visiting was done while working together.

My six brothers helped our father in the fields, and I helped our mother in the home. As soon as I was old enough, I took over the simpler jobs in order to free her for the more demanding ones. As I grew older and learned to play the piano and I became active in school and church activities, Mother would often say, "I'll dry those dishes. You go on and practice," or "I'll sew those buttons on for you. You go on to your meeting." I never objected, always finding social contacts and musical pursuits more interesting than housework. Today, as a mother of five, I still find other pursuits more interesting than housework; but, unlike my mother, I feel free to pursue my personal interests.

When I married at twenty-four, I had completed college, served a mission, and started graduate school. Having the good fortune to marry a man whose formal education was finished, I was free to complete my own graduate degree. When my second child was born, I stopped teaching freshman English and planned to devote full time to housework and mothering as my own mother had done. But except for being busy every moment of the day, my life bears little resemblance to hers. My work is surely less physically demanding—I have an automatic dishwasher, a self-cleaning oven, a self-defrosting refrigerator, an automatic washer and dryer, and nothing but wash-and-wear clothes. But my life is far from easy. One reason for this is the change of attitude in American culture that has come along with modern conveniences. Church and community leaders now seem to feel that a woman's public responsibilities needn't diminish as her house fills with children. Church assignments have seemed to increase rather than decrease with each new child. The assignments shift among Primary, Sunday School, and Relief Society, but the demands on my time remain heavy. Even the titles are not impressive. In fact, it is not the official "calls" that require the most time; it is all of the unofficial calls—to accompany a singer on the piano, to play the organ at a funeral, to organize a program, or make refreshments.

Calls from the community are almost as frequent. Young mothers are usually the only ones home to carry out such assignments as March of Dimes collections. I have declined invitations to join BYU women, a writer's guild, and the local symphony guild. But I "choked" on the "no" when it came to PTA. My concern for education and my children was too great to let that responsibility and opportunity pass me by. When I start to feel imposed upon, I look at my neighbors—one directing the girl scouts, another helping with a soccer league, another organizing the cancer drive, and I realize that I am doing no more than many Mormon mothers do.

Most of us enjoy the variety in our lives. We would be comfortable with a church job and a civic responsibility if the demands on our time stopped there. But many, like myself, hold down a part-time job as well. I have friends who cut hair, cross-guard, sew for hire, type, cook at school, or sell door-to-door. Some do it to pay for the children's braces, some for a son's mission, some for a family vacation, some even for groceries. I do it for my children's music lessons. The only way I can pay for our seven lessons is to earn enough to balance those payments. While it is something I would rather not have to do, I feel fortunate to have a skill that I can market in my own home.

My mother gave up her entire nursing career as well as her hobby of painting; I can surely give up an hour or two of each day for the musical development of my children. Perhaps I have become too much a liberated woman to suppress my ambitions. I grew up hearing that we mustn't abandon our personal growth for our families or neglect the talents we will have to use in our later lives. Perhaps I am subconsciously fighting a fear of being "trapped" as I have often felt my mother was. In any case, I began private organ study the year I gave up teaching. Then, at home with three pre-schoolers, I started playing with story plots. After a year I became serious enough about it to "make time" to work and re-work them until I had a published novel—*Elders and Sisters.* I found that my next two children were not content to sit and watch *Sesame Street* and *Mr. Rogers,* so I shelved other writing projects and gave those two hours a day to PTA work and care for my aging parents. Through it all I have clung tenaciously to my music, even though it means practicing at ten or eleven at night after the children are in bed. A Bach fugue or a Mendelssohn sonata can't really replace sleep, but the satisfaction of playing them well has added great stimulation to my life.

My mother raised an outstanding family by working with her children; I feel compelled to play with mine as well. Sometimes they have to beg me to join them in a game of Clue or Monopoly, but they seldom have to ask me twice to read them a book or to practice music with them. I accompany them to lessons, drive them to classes, and read to the younger ones each night. I have accepted that as part of my responsibility as a mother, just as my mother must have accepted her responsibility to can food and to make all that bread, butter, and salad dressing.

The result of all these diverse demands upon my time has been a busy and ever-changing schedule. I live my life by the planning calendar, faithfully making a weekly schedule each Sunday evening. Some days I have to outline an hour-by-hour schedule in order to be at all appointed places more-or-less on time. The only set routines are music lessons and scheduled meetings. I wash clothes when I notice that the hamper is full; I clean walls when the cobwebs become obvious; I organize my drawers and closets when I can no longer find what I need.

A diary entry in April 1980 showed that on a particular Friday I attended a stake Primary board meeting, practiced on an organ at BYU, taught a second-grade cooking class, played the organ for a BYU convocation, and presided over a children's recital night program. That same week I attended a kindergarten program, went visiting teaching, spoke to a local literary club, gave a presentation at a PTA meeting, planted beans, potatoes, and gladiolas in our garden, and entertained some friends. I assume that I also washed, cleaned, and cooked three meals each day and took the children to all their music lessons as well as teaching my own. I don't recall how or when, but I know it all got done.

So I go to bed at night as tired as my mother used to be, stimulated by the variety in my day, but emotionally exhausted at having to be at so many places and having to accomplish so much in so little time. For several years I found myself tense and irritable, as I remember my mother once was. My recent addiction to aerobic dance with its strenuous yet delightful workout is now a saving grace in my life, a chance to "sweat out" all tensions and pressures.

There are still other graces that make my life more than bearable. If our era has pushed the women out of the home, it has also pulled the men in. My husband not only encourages me, but he also does the dinner dishes, reads to the children, edits all my writing, and joins me in major cleaning projects.

My frustration is not so much with the number of my activities as with the limitations of a twenty-four-hour day. Many things are not done as well as I would wish because there is too little time. Yet when I seek to simplify my life, I can find nothing that I want to give up. I enjoy what I do. I still have organ recitals to give, more books to write, classes to teach, a family history project I am eager to complete, compassionate service I desire to render, friendships I want to nourish, and most important—I have five children I want to enjoy and to nurture to productive adulthood.

Once I asked my mother *how* she did it. She answered, "A day at a time." I have never dared ask *why* she did it. When I was younger, I felt that she had sacrificed unnecessarily, that she had been a martyr to the supposed welfare of her family. She *could* have bought store-made bread, ready-made soap, and dairy-churned butter. My friends' mothers did. Yet if she had been asked why she did it, I am certain the answer would have been: "I did what I had to do." Now that I understand her better, I realize that, given her life of struggle, hard work, and sacrifice, she was emotionally equipped to act in no other way. She acted well a role that seemed required of her.

Some day a granddaughter of mine with a still different approach to life may learn of my activities and ask, "How did you do it?" I will also have to answer, "One day at a time." And if she asks me why I lived such a fragmented life, why I tried to take on so many responsibilities and fill so many roles, why I submitted myself to so much pressure, I will have to reflect upon my upbringing, my personal interests, the attitudes of my time, and answer her in all honesty: "I did what I had to do—and I enjoyed it!"

Helen Candland Stark

An Underground Journey Toward Repentance

It was the first evening of a college course in magazine article writing. I felt conspicuously old and alien. Among those vibrant young people my instinct was to become invisible. I would listen and learn.

The instructor began by asking each student to suggest possible topics for research. One student announced that he hoped to do a story on the university's outstanding ROTC unit. Without warning, out boiled my response: "What about the dark side of the program? Why, it is not even Christian!" Shocked silence at this crone who had dared to kick a sacred cow! Now I was center stage with my foot in my mouth. I slumped into my chair.

Several weeks later the young man reported frustration. He had received no satisfaction from the commanding Colonel. Again I lashed out: "The Colonel is a hard-hitting propagandist who bludgeons his audience. He caused my husband to have a heart attack."

Why had I done it again? The weekend was heavy with guilt and foreboding. There I had sat before all those beautiful young people, an irascible witch, caught in the same trap I had myself decried. My thoughts circled round and round, but with the tally of the Colonel's sins mounting in my head. I bitterly recalled the party hosted by an eminent scientist at which this man was guest speaker. He had ranted long and beligerently about the urgency of total military hardware. My husband and I had come home seething with indignation, piously extolling our own peace testimony. Within the hour my husband had indeed been rushed to the hospital with a heart attack.

Actually I had never spoken with the Colonel, but I believed that I stood for higher values and that he epitomized the dark side of ecclesiastical orthodoxy: he is sanctimonious, rigid, manipulative, arrogant, and ruthless. I would gladly scratch his eyes out! I told myself that the reason he had given the young man no help was that he was planning to write a self-serving article himself. How I enjoyed believing that his halo had slipped a little. Like a child I wanted to tell God on him. But I was really frightened, too. I panicked at the thought of yet another irrational public display, yet I secretly enjoyed venting my hatred on this offensive authority figure.

Where can I go for help? I asked myself. I know of no counselor who can free me of this obsession. In such a tangle could I possibly find the end of that golden string which, as William Blake suggested, I might wind into a redemptive ball? Could my personal journal provide any help? I have sometimes used it to uncover a needed insight. At least it might move me off dead center. Suppose I set down any happening that seems to have a bearing. Perhaps I should venture underground beyond the busy mind, to toss prayerfully whatever I discover, into my own witch's cauldron.

ITEM: A death announcement in the newspaper leads me to wonder whether the Colonel might be the son of similarly named dear friends from past teaching days. They were gentle and loving persons.

ITEM: A large painting titled "Eternal Life" hangs in the Fine Arts Building foyer. It depicts two male figures (Christ and Adam?) floating around a "foetus" which is gathered into a kind of plastic bag from which a tree grows with a dove sitting on it. I find it offensive, a chauvinistic perversion, a concept of rebirth without any feminine symbol. I tell myself the Colonel, too, is totally male-oriented. An anachronism.

ITEM: A beloved teacher died today. Thinking of his wife's loss, I find lines from Tennyson keep running through my head: "—too full for sound and foam,/ When that which drew from out the boundless deep/ Turns again home." In this context my involvement with venom is like dirty foam.

ITEM: I dream of an attic full of books, people, birds. Some bad men want to release the birds but I seal up the exits, leaving only dangerous birds as in Hitchcock's film. Some visitors allow part of them to escape, not knowing such acts are off-limits. I wake up straining to remember why this dream seems to pertain to non-aggression. As a conservationist, what am I doing locking up birds? Even dark and messy ones?

ITEM: I remember a Haiku I wrote one lovely Sunday morning on the Haverford College campus. Men were spraying trees.

Sprayers rumble on.
Leaves drip poison dew. Cats prowl.
I do it with words.

ITEM: On a TV talk program candidates discuss why they ran for public office and why they lost. A personable young man with long hair and a full beard has been arrested for causes—civil rights, sit-ins. He seems humane, idealistic, dedicated, and no great threat. But a whisper campaign among some rightist groups accuses him of taking money from the Communists, being sent home from a Church mission and disfellowshipped. It occurs to me that some people look at him in the same way I see the Colonel—someone to fear.

ITEM: Today I found a hand-thrown bowl on sale in the Fine Arts Center. A soft blue glaze underlies a design, suggesting the sea or grass or clouds. Although I cringed at the price, I brought it home, only to realize that all my rooms are full of bowls.

Is there something so estranged in me that my archangel sends me out after more bowls? Are they a feminine symbol, round like the moon, a ring, a womb? They are formed on earth, the stuff that made Adam and grass. From olden times they have been shaped by the innovative cupped hand for filling and pouring.

ITEM: A young and new university president. And a lonely figure pinned against a backdrop of podium seats. Interminably. For every standee the academic procession is late and long. But for the former president, today old and ill, nothing but the characteristic iron-will keeps him upright. A man who has ruled dynamically, powerfully and, yes, ruthlessly, he now seems bound to me by ancient and mythic ties. Even he has come to this, a small broken bird in his bright red robe, pin-pointed like a forgotten drop of blood on a bright new page of history.

ITEM: An article in the Spring-Fall, 1971 issue of *Inward Light* is called "Wrestling with the Daimonic." Unlike demons, *daimons* are said to be earthly or even angelic spirits which bestir souls. The author tells of her own witch:

> Yakety yak, big mouth, saying how it all is, how it all should be, lecturing me and everybody else—arrogant, presumptuous, intrusive.

> —invite her in, sit with her at table, oh my horror my despair. It's no sin to be a black witch. (It isn't?) I'm nice to her. She weeps angrily—a pool on the floor—There's a lot of my mother karma in this witch: sarcastic, critical, demanding, perceptive, warm, hilarious, doing for others—She needs a friend, that's for sure, whether she knows it or not. Kiss her and love her. Like the hideous bride in Chaucer's "Wife of Bath Tale" she will transform.

Perhaps now I should come up from my well, hands overflowing with weeds and with treasure. I still do not understand why I find ecclesiastical and military authority so threatening, nor why I so often seek to impose my will harshly on others. These matters must be searched out further.

But I stand humbled before that alchemy which has merged my welter of positive and negative happenings into a tenuous new insight. I perceive that although nemesis does indeed follow hubris, it is not for me to force that resolution. The gods grind inexorably and in their own time. The outcome is not up to me.

Yet, it is within my province to try to understand how projecting evil intent onto another blinds my recognition of that other's divine spark. Each of us carries a drive toward wholeness, each of us struggles with outer and inner reconciliations. Each is in process of becoming truly human.

If I am far from reaching that goal, then I must go down again and again into the deep waters where the ripples widen and meld in creative darkness. There I must learn to accept injustice, paradox, pain and loneliness. If healing is to begin, I must befriend my alienated self. I must honor the creative potential within my own witch.

It would seem that as a result of even a small turning, Grace brushes by, for I one day encountered a strangely tender but undeserved epiphany.

It is the Christmas season, and the Colonel has just been retired. At a holiday festivity we find ourselves unaccountably standing beside each other. I share a precious memory from teaching days in a small mining town, when as part of the community Christmas program, I directed a one-act play, called "Why the Chimes Rang."

Starting home from the afternoon dress rehearsal, I had witnessed a sledding accident that required my taking a little girl to the hospital. There, in the emergency room, lay my small main character, his throat cut in a similar accident. As the doctor stitched him up, the boy assured me, with authority, that I was not to worry. He would do his part in the play. Above the bandages his intense face looked almost ethereal.

That evening the auditorium filled with jovial townfolk who hushed as the drama unfolded on stage—the story of the lame child with no suitable gift for the Baby Jesus—who offered his crutch when at last he stood beside the manger. The long silent church bells proclaimed the acceptance of a holy gift.

After I finish my story, there is a warm, endearing, silence. Then, "I remember it well," says the Colonel, "you see I was that little boy."

Karen Rosenbaum

For Now I See Through a Glass Darkly

When I was two-and-twenty, like Housman, only mildly cynical, I knelt one night on the concrete floor of my two-room basement apartment, and I asked for a sign of some sort that God was there, that It—was true. This prayer was not a unique one for me; I had offered it frequently in fact, especially since my male friends had begun bearing ponderous testimonies and disappearing behind white shirts, blue airletters and the ubiquitous alias "Elder." I, on the other hand, was unable to say I "knew" much of anything. I felt like a spiritual retard. It was not a comfortable feeling.

That night, as I unbent my knees, pushed aside the covers and was about to fold myself into the sheets, something caught my myopic eyes. It was a light—golden, fluted, about four feet above the floor, maybe twelve feet from my bed. A contact lens wearer, I couldn't just reach for my glasses and more closely examine this strange manifestation. An enormous tide of terror rose inside me. It did not ebb. This is it, my mind said. This is my visitation, my answer. I sat, back stiff against the metal headboard and held my breath. My brain tried to keep pace with my stampeding heart. What will I do, I thought. What will *it* do? How will it change my life? I couldn't go to sleep with it hovering there. Yet it didn't seem to be doing anything, going anywhere. Most of all, it was eerily silent. We had a standoff—it and I—for about five minutes.

I will approach it, I thought. Perhaps there is some rational explanation for this. A fiber of hope trembled inside me. I made my way around the end of the bed, my cold feet padding on the cold floor. It did not move as I came closer. It appeared immutable, invulnerable.

Finally, I decided. I would find out if it had physical parts. I reached out my hand—and I touched glass.

Glass! I felt—up, down, to both sides.

It was the door that separated my apartment from my landlord's storage room. I had lived in the apartment two months, but I had never before noticed that the top panel was glass, painted the same camel color as the rest of the door and the walls. For the first time since I had moved in, someone in my landlord's family had left on the storage room light.

As I exhaled a combined sigh and giggle and tromped back to bed, I did not feel deprived of a spiritual experience. I felt enormous relief.

To believe or not to believe that It is true or that It is only partly true—that is my dilemma, dilemma consisting of both choice and pain. The choice is limited because I did not choose to become a Mormon. I choose to try and reconcile my adult experiences with my childhood faith so that I may remain a Mormon.

Why is that reconciliation so difficult? "Aha!" says my Elihu, as comforting to me as Job's was to him. "I heard you express relief. You don't really *want* to know if It is true."

I consider that. I'm not really one for theatrics; I would rather hear still small voices than see sudden startling lights. And although I am not eager to make the enormous sacrifices and commitments that I imagine such knowledge would require, I think I could and would do so. But I admit there *are* some things that make Not Knowing attractive. Not Knowing has a lot of esthetic possibilities. Knowing suggests didacticism; didacticism usually annihilates art. Conclusion: I can write better stories out of uncertainty than I can out of dogmatism. Not Knowing is also more intellectually acceptable than Knowing—and I am part of an academic community. In theory, of course, seeking truth is essential to both the academic and the spiritual researcher. Both gather information and experiment to see if certain ideas work. The spiritual search for truth generally does not stress objective disinterest, however, while the academic search generally does. And in the academic world, seeking is safer than finding.

Yet the soul has always seemed more significant to me than the intellect; I distrust the swollen brain and the shrunken spirit. Most of the years that I have followed the prescriptions to fast, read the scriptures and then pray to know "these things" were true, I saw the proposition as quite a simple one and expected that my seed of hope would grow into a tree, or at least a respectable shrub of knowledge. It did not. And because it did not, now I am unable to hush the nagging voices in my mind. Perhaps I am invalidating the experiment, the voices say. Perhaps fasting distorts the perceptions as peyote does. Perhaps I am talking myself into believing all this. Perhaps like Pilate

I'll never know the truth. These voices—how do I keep them quiet? Is it my fault they interrupt my prayers? Do they trouble only the wicked? I can make no claims of sanctity, but apparently virtue isn't always a prerequisite for a testimony. I think of Paul.

The biggest obstacle to my faith then is the culmination of denied requests for knowledge and comfort. I do not know whether God does not speak to me or whether I do not or cannot hear. I do know that my hope has diminished. Paradoxically, decreased expectations are my way of protecting the beliefs I have. I count on less; therefore my faith will suffer less if those requests also seem to go unheard. Ironically too, it is often intellectual reasons rather than spiritual ones that hold me to the Church. I have experimented, in a scientific way, with certain principles, and they seem to me valid: our lives are better, for example, if we direct them toward others; the concept of the family is healthy and beautiful; each human being has to take responsibility for his own actions.

"Aha," Elihu says, eager to repeat what he wants to believe, "you know It is true; you just don't know that you know."

His reply, based on generous impulses, increases my distress. "You are good enough," he seems to be telling me," but your tentative testimony is not." In order for me to be an appropriate model for children, to survive a stake president's interview with my fingernails intact, to ascend to celestial serenity, I must have no doubts. I must *know*.

Echo: I don't know much of anything, but I do know that I don't know. In the other world in which I live, I am not ashamed of telling someone—a friend, a student, a colleague—"I don't know." Coupled with a subsequent search to find out, that seems to me an honorable response.

In the church world, although my search is lasting all my life, my "I don't know" is isolating and ignominious. Perhaps by writing it down, the loudest admission of it I have ever made, I have committed myself to Never Knowing. I hope not. I hope still, a hope heavy with qualifications, to see a real light, golden and fluted and not silent, but very, very soft.

"It seems a shame
that we have to learn
to grow and give . . . by practicing
on small human beings.
But I do know this:
because of my children,
I am a better human being
than I was ten years ago."
Myrna Marler

Maureen Ursenbach Beecher

Birthing

''Tomorrow we'll do it, then,'' said the obstetrician, peeling off his sterile gloves. ''Call me at 7:30 to be sure the hospital can handle us.'' With a pat to my thigh intended to convey confidence and reassurance, he left the examining room. I would not see him again until the end had begun.

We had been together, he and I, more than just the nine months of this adventure. A hesitant, no longer young bride, I had weaseled my way into his already full practice with protestations that ''if we're going to do it at all, we have to do it right away.'' He specialized in infertility, and somehow that made him worth the effort. At the pre-marital examination he had pronounced all in readiness, and then shocked sudden tears to my eyes with the announcement that ''medically I should advise you not to have children.'' He recited statistics about Down's syndrome and older mothers, backing study with study, overwhelming me in those few moments with mathematics and the moral dilemmas concurrent with amniocentesis and IUDs, with abstinence and abortion. ''Whatever you and your husband decide,'' he added, ''I'll go with you.''

Returning six months later, lab report in hand, the

pregnancy "pos" box checked, I read in his face a practical mix of congratulation and dismay—how nice, but he really didn't need one more pregnant woman this month. The dismay faded with subsequent visits. We talked of his progenitors, Pratts and Romneys they were, from the Mexican colonies, and of my work in the Church's history division, writing accounts of just such stalwarts as his ancestors. Of the pregnancy there was little mention; things were "progressing nicely," and I was given to understand that the complaints that went with my condition were simply to be endured. Was I not, after all, a daughter of Eve in sorrow bringing forth my children, I thought angrily after one more visit diminished, again, my hopes for relief from the interminable nausea. "Doesn't the Benedictin work?" sympathized the nurse.

Now at last the pregnancy would be over. Back at my office I had cleared my desk before leaving for the appointment; colleagues there would be pleased not to see me tomorrow.

By eight the next morning we were at the admissions desk. "Yes?" asked a white starched nurse. "I'm here to have a baby," I explained. She led me off for the routines which hospitals impose on people who come there. I had never had an enema before.

By the time Dale had filed the admission forms with the computer-head of the hospital, I was gowned and bedded in a narrow room surrounded by a bank of monitors. Competent people began attaching me by various cords to the hospital machinery: the intravenous first, to my arm, then the plastic tube to my spine. I welcomed that one, having been reassured by my doctor that, since we were too busy for breathing lessons, and since he fully expected me to demand some anesthetic when it would be too late to inject it, why not plan on the epidural block. It will be nice, I thought, to be awake but numb.

"Will you sign here, please," smiled the young resident as he pushed a clip board toward my I.V.'d arm. "Your doctor has agreed to let you be part of our study." I was getting used to being a guinea pig, but Dale had questions. "Oh, there's nothing experimental in the pill itself," the resident explained. "We just need to know how much dosage at what stage is best for inducing labor." Dale signed, I swallowed, and the process was made immediately irreversible, despite nervous jokes of "Are you sure you want to go through with this?"

From some intern's sleeve appeared a white plastic device resembling an outsized crochet hook. "Just to break the sac," he explained, as though invading private space were nothing at all. Two more cords wired me to the machinery of the system. The fetal monitor beeped encouragingly, and, hardly minutes after my ingestion of the pill, the swinging arm of the second monitor began to indicate contractions. "Here comes one," Dale would say. "Shut up," I thought. The pain surged through my abdomen, swelling to an intensity I had never experienced, then relenting. "Just tell me when it starts to peak out, will you?" I hoped that he wouldn't feel rejected that I didn't want his warnings. Bonding between husband and wife during labor was important, the book had said.

In the spaces between, I tried to think of other things, but birthing will not be upstaged. The scene from a B-rated movie played across my thoughts, an Indian woman, crouching and grunting in a copse of aspen and then emerging impossibly soon after, her children bundled in her skirts, to present her son to his father. Too neat, I thought. Then I remembered another Indian birthing story that seemed, in comparison, genuine. In a lecture series on women's issues, a Navajo nurse-social worker had been an invited panelist. I recalled nothing of her assessment of the medical problems of Indian women, but remembered having been deeply moved by her account, told and retold in familiar ways, of the birth of her father.

It was so different then, there, to that mother, Hasbah, birthing her fourth child in a hogan. None of the impersonal white sterility of this hospital, none of the tubes and wires which even now linked me to systems I might never need. Only the red cord sash which the medicine man had tied to the sacred west beam of the hogan for Hasbah to cling to when the pains came hard.

None of the white-suited mob of unknown faces was here; instead her oldest daughter, watching over the coffee can boiling on the oil drum stove, assuring the cleanliness of the pocket knife with which the cord would be cut, the string with which it would be tied; her husband, in and out of the hogan as he dug the oval hole in the first floor in front of the sheepskins which were the delivery mat; her mother, rubbing between her hands the cedar bark—soft, very soft, for the baby's diaper—and placing it on the sheepskin blanket; Old Man Manygoats, his blessingway chants, slow, monotonous, rhythmic, singing the baby out. And finally, her uncle, his strong arms around her waist giving gentle downward pressure. Everyone loved and loving, each involved intimately in the event now taking place on the birthing mat. Another contraction, a hard one; Hasbah grabbed the sash belt. Her mother coached her on. She grunted as she pushed again. She let her baby come gently, her mother helping, expert and smooth with her hands. A son. The vigorous cry filled the hogan. The grandmother laid the baby in the fluffy sheepskin. She wiped his face and back. Old Man Manygoats sang the chant of the corn pollen boy. Grandmother cut the cord and tied it. She wrapped the baby and gave him to his mother's breast. My eyes teared in anticipation of my own coming moment.

"She's crowning!" bellowed the nurse, having once more invaded that space no longer private. "Where's the doctor?" "Didn't *you* call?" "Oh, damn." "Well, let's take her into delivery."

By the time Dale returned, gowned and scrubbed, I was lost in my own body, in a world I had never known so well. The epidural block had not worked—it had seemed odd that deadened pain should be so fierce—but I was above caring. I felt the muscles move to my command. I pressed, relaxed, and pressed again, moving all the world in my own belly. I felt the baby press, I panted "not yet," I held him for the moment, confined in the birth canal, while some functionary did his thing with the scalpel. He signalled his completion of the episiotomy. Now! I opened, pressed, and eased my child from the moist darkness of my body into the dry brightness of this unfriendly world. We would meet later, I promised, and I would make it up to him.

They whisked him away, out of range of my astigmatic vision. Across the room I could make out wild thrashing arms and legs in the isolette. "Go at it, baby. You've waited a long time for that."

I was glad the delivery room crew had other things to do, that Dale had places to look. The grin on my face, I knew, must be grotesque. I wrapped my arms around myself and closed my eyes. Dale left to share his happy news at the office.

The recovery room nurse was a soul from the past,

ministering supreme in this roomful of women. A nineteenth-century midwife, I mused to myself, as she calmly went from mother to newer mother with her homely comforts, her warm messages. The lace of her Mormon garment through the white uniform seemed somehow anachronistic—Patty Sessions would have had plainer. But her ministrations were as caring as those of the midwife.

She could have delivered my baby, I thought, remembering other midwives I had read about. It would have been comforting to have spent a confinement among such women, to have been blessed by them. A sacred washing and anointing of women before their delivery had been common even up to the time of my own birth. I wondered if warm Relief Society hands had pressed their blessings on my mother's modest body, if the fetus that was to become me had felt the surge of spirit from those sacred words.

I had earlier found the text of such a blessing, carefully penned into the Relief Society minutes book nearly a century ago. There at my desk in the church archives, cars humming by outside my window, I had read the blessing. Parts of it reverberated now:

> . . . we wash you preparatory to your safe delivery and speedy recovery, for life, health, salvation, for yourself and your offspring, asking God the Eternal Father that His holy spirit may attend this ordinance.

There were blessings for each member of the body, for each function, all articulated in a blend of the practical and the sublime utterance:

> . . . that every cord and muscle may be strong and healthy, that the marrow of your bones [be] warmed up by the spirit of God. . . . That your heart might be comforted and that no cold might settle upon [your] bosom and that your milk may be pure and filled with nourishment.

Anticipating what had been a most serious threat to my sisters in the past, the blessing prayed against premature delivery.

> that [your womb] might be strengthened and the ligaments thereof that it may retain what is there-in deposited to its full time and bring forth in perfection.

How easily such concepts had slipped from the lips of nineteenth-century Saints: perfection was for the gods, I had often reminded myself.

> We ask that your child might be perfect in every limb and joint and muscle . . .

And so would he be, my child?

> That it might be beautiful to look upon, that its nerves may be strong, that it may be happy in its spirit, . . . that it may be free from spot or blemish, that it may be filled with faith from its mother's womb.[2]

The holy blending of the magnificent and the mundane that is a woman's blessing had poured over me, and I felt the strength of sharing, the continuity of sisterhood. The office secretary, poking her head into my alcove, had wondered at the water on my cheeks. Someday I would tell her of the washings of love which span decades.

Now, ecstatic beyond sleep, I was moved readily back to my room, watching, as I passed, my name being erased from the blackboard now filled with names of others in a long listing of delivery room comings and goings. In the bed adjacent lay my roommate. Two beds opposite were empty. After not much preliminary talk with my neighbor, I sensed some deep grief beyond her telling. When the nurse arrived with the woman's baby, I knew. "She doesn't look funny, does she?" the mother pleaded. The lower ears, the slanted eyes. "No, of course not," I answered. I did not lie. She had a new born loveliness that Down's syndrome could not alter. The baby's father came in, in his bishop's voice playing out complacencies about this "special angel," this seventh child whose difference neither parent had in the slightest anticipated. He left his wife uncomforted.

Into the evening we talked, she and I. I had read some things she needed to know, and she had some fear, some anger, but mostly a bottomless sorrow which she could barely speak. To be a mother so many times, secure in her skills, and then to find herself dependent on a nurse to be taught how to feed a child who cannot synchronize the sucking with the swallowing. She was where I was, having to learn first hand the mother things.

Underneath it all, the talking and listening, lay in me an urgency which finally burst out. "Oh, I wish they'd bring my baby!" I cried. "Why didn't you say?" my new friend replied. "I'll call the nursery for you."

George came in with the wheeled crib. Our friend, as well as pediatrician, he was a welcome sharer in this first holding of my first born. "He's beautiful," George announced, "and normal." Then, in very doctory tones, he instructed, explained, assured. Touching the baby's hand in parting, he hesitated. "Maureen, look," he said. "This line on his palm is continuous. Down's babies often have that." Tears sprang. Through many months afterward I would caress that line, reminded of the healthy mind with which our Daniel had been blessed, of how easily it could have been otherwise.

George left, my roommate turned to sleep, and the nursery attendant, after a brisk warning not to risk falling asleep with the baby in my arms, left us. Now at last, was the moment of my peace. The nameless child fit himself into the crook of my arm as he had so many months nested in the warmth of my womb. Only now there was no squirming, no jabbing of leg or arm, no eagerness for separation. Oh, this is better, we seemed to say to each other. And I resented the others, the ever-present others, who had until now kept us from this moment.

Why the coldness of it all, why the white sterility, the metalic intrusions into our process? The machines, the strangers, the unfamiliar walls. Reason intervened: what if things had not gone so well? What if you needed instruments? or oxygen? How many babies had been saved because of the warnings of a fetal monitor? Or delivered Caesarean when things went wrong? Infant mortality among nineteenth-century Mormon women was about ten percent; the facts injected themselves into my reverie.

The midwives, for all their comforting presence, had been helpless in so many cases. Juanita Brooks had written of Grandma Leavitt, midwife in the remote Mormon community on the Arizona strip. The birthing was not going well, once, and there was no earthly help beyond the midwife's own experience. Theresa Leavitt provided the details:

> Grandma was called to Littlefield to take care of Alice Strausser Knight, wife of Edward Knight, with her first baby. She could see that she must have help, so she sent Theresa for some Elders, and she brought back the two Frehner brothers, Albert and Henry.
>
> They administered to her, but still things were not working right, so she sent Theresa to get Harmon Wittwer and Parley Hunt who were camped by the school house on their way north with a load of salt. It was in the middle of the night, but Theresa woke

> them and told them they were needed badly over at Knight's.
>
> Now there were four men all holding the Melchizedek Priesthood kneeling around her bed and asking for the Lord's help. Grandma said she wanted everyone to take part in prayer, one after another, and not to stop praying until this child is born.
>
> Only one or two had prayed when she stopped us. "Something is wrong here," she said. "Someone in this group has hard feelings against each other, and I want them to make it right so that we can be united and the Spirit of the Lord made manifest and this child can be born."
>
> No one said a word for a few seconds, and then brothers Albert and Henry Frehner got to their feet and said they had a bitter quarrel that day, and were not speaking to each other. They stood there and with tears in their eyes asked each other's forgiveness.
>
> Then they all kneeled again, and the praying went on, but not for long. These two brothers had hardly finished before the baby was born.[3]

That was the backup support, I realized. Priesthood. And I had known that, too. Early in the pregnancy, when the nausea was preventing me from the level of productivity my work required, Dale had blessed me through his priesthood privilege. I had already learned to listen carefully to his words—they were short, simple and, experience had demonstrated, either inspired or confirmed from above. This blessing, going beyond what I thought was my need—to be able to do my work—pronounced almost as an afterthought that "the baby is healthy." That was all, but it was enough. Fears of Down's syndrome left me, and I was free for the rest of my term to anticipate in peace the birth of my normal baby boy. Amniocentesis could have told as much, I realize, but this was better for me. My own intuition—I had not even bothered listing girls' names among the boys'—and Dale's pronouncement had replaced mystery with knowledge, fear with comfort.

So this was birthing, this crazy-quilt of contrasts, of senses and feelings in chaos, coming occasionally to rest, as now, with a sleeping son in the crook of my arm. Had I won the grand prize? or was there a bigger and better one behind another curtain? Hasbah, Alice Knight, the women washed and anointed, the ones with surgical deliveries, my roommate, did they have it better? or even different? So much we had shared: the sisterhood of women at birthing times; the practical rituals, pleasant or unpleasant, necessary or unnecessary; the religious rites and their invoking of the divine; our private moments of self-knowledge, when, by whatever process our bodies have borne their burden; and the public acknowledgement of the oneness of the human family.

And I had known it all. Had experienced the sisterhood, had participated in a ritual as old as seeding wheat, had sensed the link, to powers beyond my own, had found my own soul, had felt God.

---

[1]Ursula Wilson, "Tom Knocki, Son of Hasbah," from a panel presentation 20 November 1975 in "Utah Women: Roots and Realities" series. Notes in the author's files.

[2]Oakley Second Ward Relief Society Minutes, 1901-1910, Church Archives, Historical Department, The Church of Jesus Christ of Latter-day Saints, Salt Lake City, Utah.

[3]Theresa Leavitt, as quoted in Juanita Brooks, "Mariah Huntsman Leavitt: Midwife of the Desert Frontier," in *Forms upon the Frontier: Folklife and Folk Arts in the United States,* edited by Austin Fife, *et al.* (Logan, Utah: Utah State University Press, 1969). pp. 125-26.

Judith Rasmussen Dushku

Time of Decision

"You are Pro-Choice aren't you?" mumbled the young legislator at his desk as he pored over my application. Anticipating my response, he wrote the label boldly across the front page. I asked why the label had to be so prominently displayed on my application for a seat on the Massachusetts Delegation to the White House Conference on Families.

"Come on," he replied sarcastically. "You know this game. When we had the state elections, the Pro-Lifers were so well organized they walked all over the delegate selection process. They bused in hundreds of voters every day. Almost all the delegates were from their slates. We checked them out. Some are reasonable people—an asset to the state—but some are real crazies. The Governor is upset. He is a Pro-Lifer, as you know, but he is embarrassed by this mob. Even he admits that the delegation needs balance. So now he wants a list to choose his appointees from. Probably he will name more Pro-Lifers, but he would like a list of decent minorities and decent Pro-Choice types to pick from. I just heard you were pregnant. Can I tell him? Pro-Choice and pregnant is easier to take than just Pro-Choice." He took a quick breath and began again.

"These right-wingers are so prepared for battle they had their buses loaded while we were still putting a staff together. I give them credit for enthusiasm, but they are the scariest people I've ever met. I'm a good Catholic with a clean Pro-Life record, but they call me names because I talk to people like you. Sorry—

"Anyway, *that* is why I have to know where you stand and I have to make it public." I started to protest but he went on. "Yeah, it's too bad. I know some people like to keep their thoughts on abortion to themselves. It's a heavy issue. But these days you have to take a stand—publicly.

"Hey, what's the matter? I thought you *were* a Pro-Choice person. Someone from NOW and from your university said you are a real civil-liberties type and a supporter of the State Women's Caucus. No?"

Of course I am Pro-Choice, I reminded myself. Hadn't I always believed in freedom and agency for all? I had been teaching civil liberties to my political science classes for thirteen years, working hard to impress upon students the value of guaranteeing this freedom. It was a philosophy that had never embarrassed me. Although it is a hard principle to apply in all situations, I have never questioned it as a good and right goal. Moreover, it is a basic tenet of my religion. Growing up a Mormon I had been taught the principle of free agency, and I have always taken it seriously. People—all people—have the right and responsibility to choose.

Yes, I had read President Kimball's strong statement on abortion, and I felt that I understood his counsel. A society that encourages abortions does tend to lose sight of the value of human life and does begin to feel less responsibility for the conceiving and the bearing of children. But

I had never understood his counsel to negate individual agency.

"Of course," I responded firmly to the legislator. "Put my name on the top of your 'Decent Pro-Choice' list!"

Although I was not appointed by the Governor of Massachusetts, I was picked by a White House team from a pool of at-large nominees and sent to the Conference on Families in Baltimore in May 1980, where I associated myself with the Pro-Choice faction.

I liked most of them. They were good people, seemingly dedicated to improving institutions that affect family life. Although this group constituted a clear numerical majority at the Conference, it incurred the constant wrath of the vocal and critical "minority representing the Moral Majority" who claimed mistreatment at the hands of everyone else.

I met several Mormons at the Conference. They were tenatively friendly but suspicious of my lack of the identifying buttons or banners of the Moral Majority. I had counted on my maternity dress to endear me to them. When two fervent women asked me how I could possibly refrain from endorsing a like-minded people committed to "all" the same things "we" were, I replied, "I don't believe that they *are* committed to all of the goals of the Church. In fact, I see some of their efforts as *conflicting* with the goals of my church." One woman shook my hand and left. Another discussed points of disagreement for a few minutes, frowned, as if she were sure the Spirit had departed my soul, then backed away with a promise to send me some literature. I was left to my thoughts.

My thoughts had to do with choosing—choosing the best as opposed to the better, the bad as opposed to the worst, choosing the great over the simply worthwhile.

Speakers at the Conference clarified some of my thoughts and confused others. Each proclaimed some policy as essential, and each was convincing. Once preliminary policy recommendations had been agreed to, I and the other delegates had to mark ballots showing whether or not we "agreed strongly," "agreed moderately," "disagreed strongly" or "disagreed moderately." At first I tried to imagine myself in the place of those making the proposals, but I soon gave up on that. It was hard enough to decide what I would do for myself.

The more I thought about these choices, the more agonizing the process seemed. I began to favor policies that enlarged the scope of choice. It seemed important that each human being have the right to make his or her own choices without interference.

A handicapped delegate took the floor to propose that the conference go on record as supporting laws in all states that would keep a handicapped person from being institutionalized, even temporarily, against his will. That seemed right. Handicapped people also have the right to choose. But the parent of a severely handicapped child spoke in opposition. He described his difficulties in rearing a family of six children with most of the money and energy spent on the one handicapped child. Because of the problems of transporting this child, the family had never taken a trip together, had never found a suitable place to leave the child or a suitable person to care for him.

"We need a break," this father said desperately. "Our child will never agree to stay in an institution, even for a few weeks. We need someone to take him—against his will —and we need the option of a family vacation!" That too was reasonable. I felt so sympathetic that I formulated a standard in my head: "The greatest number of choices for the greatest number of people."

Feeling comfortable with this, I realized that it would require decent, even inspired people to make right choices. In any system allowing a large number of options there will be selfish, careless people who will insist on hurting themselves and others. But I wanted to believe in those with imagination and compassion who were capable of doing great things for themselves and others. But I also believed that all the creativity and good will in the world are useless without the freedom to exercise them.

Our group decided to vote against the proposal on the handicapped because it would destroy too many options.

As I had expected, many speakers raised abortion issues. Since in Massachusetts the subject had been part of a long and angry debate, I thought I had heard all arguments both for and against it. But the tough questions I thought I had answered long ago were before me again. Listening to the speakers, I secretly prayed I would never have to make the decisions some of them had faced. I was to remember that prayer.

A woman with a disabled husband and four children had taken a job the week her youngest entered first grade. With her first decent paycheck, she rented an apartment larger than the three rooms they had occupied for eight years. For the first time she could look forward to a pleasant life with her family. Then unintentionally she became pregnant. Unable to obtain a legal abortion, she used her second paycheck to fly out of the country for an illegal one: "I knew my family could not stand the burden of another child."

This woman's decision reminded me of an exchange after a stake meeting. Joan A. had said how sad it was that Sister Y. had not known she was carrying a severely retarded baby, a baby that was now bringing great hardship to its family. A listening stake leader sternly reprimanded Joan for implying that there might have been a righteous alternative to having the child. His own sister had also borne a retarded child and had benefitted from the situation. "It has been a marvelous learning experience for the whole family," he said. When questioned later, however, he admitted that in some ways this "learning experience" had been disastrous. The father suffered a nervous breakdown; the two children went into therapy; the mother lapsed into depression; and the couple finally divorced. The stake leader allowed that the family might have been spared these unfortunate things if it had not been blessed with a handicapped child.

I pursued the discussion. The spirit in the handicapped body could have entered a different body with an alternative set of blessings. Parents are obliged to do all they can to provide for the spiritual as well as the physical well-being of spirits entrusted to them. Just as a parent should take advantage of medical science to protect the health of a child after birth, so should that same parent take pains to provide the healthiest possible bodies for the spirits of the unborn.

The leader's testimony was unmoved. The Lord had intended his sister to bear her handicapped child. But he admitted that he did find my speculations troublesome and discomforting. When I thought of all three sisters at once—the one in Baltimore with the abortion, the one in our stake with the new baby, and the leader's sister—I too was troubled.

During the rest of my time at the Conference, certain truths came to me forcefully and unexpectedly, with new and deeper meaning. In the past I had heard and had repeated to myself a whole set of judgments on the importance of having children, the greatness of blessings bestowed upon women who participate in the sacred process of giving birth. Somehow, however, my experience seemed rather routine. To be sure, I had regarded the birth of a child, mine or someone else's, as miraculous, but I had never given the event the reverence I was now realizing it deserved. The addition of each child to our family had never required significant sacrifice on anyone's part, I thought. Imagining other circumstances was shocking me into a new level of awareness. The preparation—physical and spiritual—that must often accompany the bringing of a helpless child into a hostile world can be arduous. It is important to use wisdom in choosing if and when to have a child at any time or place. Granted the standards for making wise judgments may change, wisdom must prevail. For the first time I realized that part of being a wise and a good mother was choosing when to have a child and how many children to have.

Thinking again of the stake leader's sister, I found myself respecting her for her efforts to make the birth of the child a growth experience for herself and her family. But I realized too that I would have respected her if she had chosen *not* to bear the child, thus sparing them the trauma that followed. Life had never seemed so complicated! Motherhood especially had never seemed so serious and so difficult. Neither my motherhood nor anyone else's motherhood was as simple as it had seemed.

I was exhausted. From childhood I had anticipated a time when I might be challenged to step over a line and be counted. I had imagined myself bounding boldly to the Right Side, confident and proud, firm in my convictions. At this conference, I had taken a stand consistent with my deepest convictions. But the dramatic stepping over the line was far less satisfying than I had imagined. I found myself longing for the comfort of my private life.

Five days later I was home. Instead of comfort, however, I found a stormier scene than the one I had left in Baltimore. After a week with the children and a week away from me, my husband had confirmed for himself what he had hinted at earlier. We must *not* under any circumstances add the baby I was expecting to our large and demanding family. He was sure he could not take it. He was sure I could not take it. "Make an appointment with the doctor immediately and terminate the pregnancy," he insisted. "Neither you nor I can possibly devote the time and energy to our other children or to each other that is required if we have another baby. You must do this for the family." Although my husband is not LDS, he reminded me that a basic principle of my faith is the preeminence of the family. I was ignoring that principle.

I burst into tears as he went on. "What about the position you so boldly defended at the Family Conference?" he demanded. "You have spent all this time and energy fighting for the right of a woman to an abortion. Now you have the chance to take advantage of that right."

What followed were the most agonizing days of my life. I spent hours examining doctrines, arranging priorities, trying to understand fears and analyze anxieties. Since I am not one to suffer in silence, I shared my ambivalence with others, men and women, friends in and outside the Church. Often my cries brought demonstrations of support. Just as often I was censured for even thinking about aborting a fetus which some claimed was like "killing a child." These friends trusted me with a large number of confidences, their tales only adding to my unrest. Some had chosen to abort, others had chosen birth, some seemed sad or angry. Most of them were caring people with whom I felt real kinship of spirit.

I spent intense hours in prayer and intense hours with

my bishop. I discussed my dilemma with two therapists and several doctors and nurses. My sympathetic bishop thought I was worrying in the right way. The Lord, the Prophet, and he, my bishop, were concerned with nothing less than my eternal welfare and that of my husband—indeed of my whole family, born and unborn. President Kimball's strongly worded cautions against aborting a baby without careful, even agonizing thought and prayer, reminded me of my responsibilities. I was accountable. I could not abrogate that accountability.

Assuming that the problem of whether or not we could "handle another baby" might be less complicated if we could be assured of a normal one, I decided to undergo amniocentesis. This was intended to relieve my husband of anxiety about a handicapped child. While I found the test an intellectual delight (I am impressed with the technology of modern science), and the results delightful (I was carrying a healthy girl, our first after three sons)—my husband was not comforted. For him the issue was not the health of the child but the fact of the child itself. He and I are both forty years old. I teach fulltime at a university, and he teaches and counsels inner-city children who make enormous demands upon him. We have always been committed to doing as much as we can not only for own children but for the students we daily serve. He could not be the parent he wanted to be and still fulfill his commitments at school. I could not argue; his reasoning was sound, but I was realizing openly what I had always known secretly: I could not abort this child. Why? I certainly did not believe that to abort a fetus was murdering a child. Yet it was clear that I had already projected a lifetime of dreams, of mother-daughter intimacies upon it, calling it by name and talking to it. Was it because this would be my first daughter after three sons? Was it because of my age and the feeling that the end of my child-bearing years was near? Did I want one final chance to savor and cling to this ability? Obviously one cannot equate the long, involved problems of child-rearing with the self-contained glories of childbirth. Was I responding to fantasies of ghostly pioneer role models? Was my eternal optimism getting the better of me, leading me to disaster? Occasionally I felt inspired. My daughter was to fill a special mission in life, a mission that had been entrusted to my stewardship.

But more often I just felt unsure. It was hard to insist to my husband that the Lord was influencing me. Was I simply afraid of abortion? Yes, but not extremely so. In one ambivalent moment, I even decided to make an appointment for abortion. When I went in to see the doctor about it, the nurse asked me why. I explained that my husband felt strongly about it. She wanted to know how I felt. I admitted that I was not exactly thrilled with the idea. But it had to be; I was resigned. After describing the details of the procedure, she said, "You are a poor candidate for an abortion—at least this one. My experience has convinced me that women should not choose abortion to please their husbands or anyone else. It ruins relationships." My mouth dropped open as she went on. "It builds future resentments. You would be setting your husband up as the thief, the one who deprived you of your joy."

"Does my joy show so much?" I whispered.

"It certainly does. And your feelings of happiness are an important reason to reconsider." Although she went on to apologize for interfering, she ended with an emphatic, "Don't do it!"

By then I was sobbing. I seemed to feel several emotions at once: sadness for my husband, guilt and remorse for our relationship, terror at what I had almost done.

And joy! I realized then that I adored my unborn child in ways I could not name. I felt sure that the next few years would be harder than the last year had been, but in a strange way I was glad.

Ambivalence was to return and sleepless nights, but the clarity of that moment was to sustain me. And as an LDS woman, I desperately wanted to know whether that moment was the result of the inspiration of the Holy Spirit. I earnestly prayed for this assurance.

Although my husband had always accompanied me to the delivery room and supported me there, he was not present for the birth of our little girl. For a few weeks after she and I returned from the hospital, he felt no genuine happiness in her presence. He finally warmed to her, though, and over the past months has fallen sincerely in love with her. But our year of animosity has left deep scars on our marriage, and I worry about our daughter, indeed about our sons as well. Can we parents provide them with the spiritual sustenance they need?

Recently I met a man from the Massachusetts delegation to the White House Conference. "Ah, I remember you," he said. "You are the Pro-Choice lady."

"Yes," I replied. "I was and am for the right to choose."

I said this with such firmness that it surprised me. But I knew how long and hard I had struggled to come to this conclusion. My firm conviction was born out of a difficult struggle. But now when I heard the question I felt sure of my response. Suddenly I felt that I had had this same clear feeling before, over the same tough issue. I pondered and decided that perhaps it was during the War in Heaven when I had finally opted to come to earth, with all the uncertainties guaranteed by that decision. Yes, I had known then how hard it would be to wonder and worry through life's choices, to make mistakes and try again to be correct, and yet I had volunteered for life. With all the ambiguities I knew that I would face I had understood and known that it was right and good to do. I had been for choice then, too.

Myrna Marler

Midnight on Mothers Day

Midnight of another Mothers Day and I am wide awake. My husband baked me a cake, decorating it with cartoon drawings of our four sons, and each of my boys gave me a dutiful peck and a hug; but, as I lie here staring at the Hawaiian night sky, counting the stars between the swaying palm fronds, I feel hypocritical. I may look the part, sitting there in Church with my family so neatly lined up between my husband and me, but somehow I don't seem to be cast in quite the same mold as all those other mothers eulogized from the pulpit today.

Maybe it is because I wasn't born motherly like so many of those other mothers who shepherd their tightly organized flocks into the pews. Even as a teenage babysitter I was a poor surrogate for absentee parents. Unlike my girlfriends who pocketed untold wealth every weekend, I never took along games for the kiddies, didn't read to them and if they cried, turned up the television set. Parents, sensing this lack of nurturing yearnings in me, didn't often call. I didn't blame them.

Strangely enough, the children seemed to like me, but I tired quickly of their company. Frankly, their conversation bored me. One day riding home on a city bus, I watched unnoticed while a man talked endlessly to a little girl about her new dress, her new purse, and how her daddy was going to take her to the park. The mother beside her beamed as each lisping syllable dropped from her prodigy's mouth. Is this motherhood then, I asked myself, long days spent in the company of immature minds? At that moment I was aware of fear, fear that a good Mormon girl isn't supposed to have, a fear so alarming that I shoved it to the back of my mind and didn't examine it again until it was too late.

My generation was just on the verge of the Women's Movement. The year I married, Betty Friedan's *The Feminine Mystique* was a very recent bestseller. Though I had worked at an interesting job for several years and had supported myself until the age of twenty-four, I don't think I ever saw myself as a career girl. I was only someone waiting for the right man to come along. I also wanted very much to live the Gospel, which to me meant accepting without question the dogma that children were to come into a family often and quick. I married a man with the same kind of commitment, a man who would never have considered fathering less than six, no matter what the income or the stress level. To both of us having many babies was a way of proving our faith to the Lord. Thus, only nine months after the wedding, I was pregnant.

Excitement carried me through the first weeks until morning sickness reintroduced me to reality. Glimmerings of apprehension warned me then that my life had swung out of control, that the course I had set for myself was irreversible. I wanted the baby—of course I did—but now the choice was gone. One day I stuffed a sofa pillow under my dress to see what my body would look like come spring. Quickly I pulled the pillow out and tossed it back on the couch, willing myself to forget what I had just seen in the mirror and feeling an unexpected horror at such a deformity. And yet, as the days passed, and my waist thickened and my stomach bulged just a little more, I would press myself with curious fingers, searching for recognizable parts of a tiny body. Upon discovering the unmistakable shape of an arm or a leg, I felt a thrill of awe so profound it became almost more difficult to acknowledge than my fear. A human being was growing inside me! And I was growing big—big as the sofa pillow had prophesied—and bigger. I grew so uncomfortable that finally I said in my witty way, "Anything, anything at all, is better than this—even having a baby."

At the time I was going to beat the odds and die in childbirth—and with every pregnancy since, the thought has more than crossed my mind, has come to stay, lodged in my brain like a niggling, nagging, unwanted guest. Breathing was such an effort those last few weeks, and my pulse pounded so rapidly every time I climbed the stairs or pushed the vacuum cleaner that I knew my heart could never stand the additional strain of labor. In my unconfided fear, I visualized a full-scale funeral with mourners standing over my grave more easily than I could imagine bringing home a squalling infant to place in the empty bassinet. Since my rational self knew my fears were ridiculous, I turned them into another joke, "It's not the labor I'm afraid of," I would say to my girlfriends. "It's the dying." We would laugh, pretending that death is never a part of childbirth. Somehow my heart stood the strain and after a dreamlike interval, I heard the gasp of life entering the tiny body and then the enraged cries of my newborn son. When they placed him in my arms, he looked just as peculiar as all other newborns. My mental plans had been to care tolerantly for the infant the first three months, then, when it started to turn cute, to love it. But as I looked at his battered little head, all pushed out of shape, the purple face with eyes squeezed shut against the light as he bellowed, the tongue flickering in and out between the toothless gums, my heart surrendered to his helplessness. "Oh my darling," I said, "don't cry. It's all right."

How I loved that tiny baby! My fears changed to anxiety that something dreadful would happen to him and I would lose that fragile scrap of humanity. I could not let him sleep without checking his breathing every ten minutes. I held him by the hour, wanting him to sense and know from the beginning that he was loved. As I rocked him, I thought of a sixteen-year-old boy in the ward, clean-cut, smart, attentive to duty, courteous to his elders—all the things I wanted in my son. And I would give it all to him through my love alone.

My heart still surrenders to Jeffrey's vulnerabilities, but our relationship has not been what I visualized in those early days. I never dreamed then that the same little infant would some day be able to infuriate me to the point of physical violence. Oh yes, I had heard other mothers say, "I could have just killed him" or had seen them sigh or even yell with impatience and frustration, but those impressions had registered only vaguely on my consciousness. Those signs, those tears I was convinced were never going to impinge on my reality because so far I had kept *all* the commandments. But Jeffrey taught me all about my own vulnerabilities. By his second year he was playing in the toilet, dumping cans of grease on the newly-waxed kitchen floor, shattering irreplaceable wedding presents, scaling stoves and counters with enviable agility, finding sharp knives and waving them at imaginary windmills, and finally one day breaking a dozen fresh eggs over his baby brother's tiny head.

When Jeffrey was six months old, sleeping through the night and holding his own bottle, my husband said, "Jeffrey is so much fun. Let's have another one." I agreed because I was still ignorant of how difficult it would be to handle the active toddler that Jeffrey would become while we lived in a too-small apartment. I had no way of knowing that Aaron was going to be a demanding, crying, wide-awake baby. Besides, I wanted to show the Lord that I was willing to give and to give unstintingly. That sacrifice, I reasoned, would be in lieu of other adversities I hoped not to experience, a sacrifice certain to purify me for the Celestial Kingdom. In a way I suppose I was bargaining with God: I'll have many children, just as I'm supposed to, if You'll keep death and disaster away.

It was a revelation to me as my children started to grow older that they had developed characteristics "my" children were never going to have—that is, they were brats. They whined, declared my dinners were yucky, and refused to take baths. Where I had envisioned a gathering around the piano in the evenings, they fought at the dinner table and threw themselves down hypnotized in front of the television set. They teased each other, poked each other, hit each other, twisted each other's ears, tattled on each other, and when in public, acted as if they had never even met.

"No loyalty," I wept to my husband. "No family unity." He patted my back, uttering soothing words, but he couldn't really comfort me because all final judgments lie in the future. How will the children turn out in the end?

Subconsciously I had envisioned our life as being much like "The Brady Bunch" on television (also the picture I gleaned from the *Ensign* and Relief Society manuals). In the show, after Child storms out of the room and slams a door upstairs, Father draws a deep breath, summoning patience, then saunters after, knocks on the door, enters to find Child *sprawled on the bed and ready to talk.* Father wisely solves Child's problem and both descend to a happy conclusion. Unfortunately, I don't have television writers working for me. I, too, let the child slam off while summoning patience, but often my hands are buried in bread dough. By the time I am free enough to saunter towards the bedroom, I hear breakage behind the closed door. If he lets me in, I become immediately upset at the chaos he's created. Any chance at a *teaching moment* disappears as I feel the clutch of resentment and anger without the willpower to shrug it off.

My life has not been lived like the Brady Bunch because I didn't realize and no one had ever told me what a hard, high pressure job it is to raise children. Somehow in Sacrament Meeting and Family Home Evening and Youth Conference and Relief Society, I learned that I was simply to *have* the children—not that I needed to prepare for them, or even to take my time about producing them. People blithely informed me that I would grow with my children, but they never told me I wouldn't grow fast enough to keep up with their unremitting demands. And Relief Society was no help. It was there I realized that Super Mom lives! She comes to Relief Society and *Shares Her Experiences*, with the basic purpose, no doubt, of uplifting us all, yet with the result of pulling me down. Even though I'm working to the limit of my spiritual, emotional and physical capacities, I'm not Super Mom. My children are not achievers in school; they fight and hit each other and the neighbors, turn family outings into free-for-all, don't take care of their possessions. We don't organize family work programs, weed the garden together, or gather around the piano in the evening. And so I walk around from church meeting to church meeting oppressed first by guilt and inadequacy, finally by resentment.

And then we decided to move to Hawaii. I had imagined myself strolling down the beach in a bathing suit, but I now knew I would be waddling along the sand in a maternity dress, and I resented this pregnancy more than ever. Trying to settle in a new place, the change of climate, of altitude, the humidity, all served to give me a racking case of the miseries. Every night I sobbed on my husband's shoulder, "Oh I hate being pregnant. I can't wait until this is over!" Never have I felt so much in bondage to my own body. Every week at church people asked, "How much longer?"

Then one day the doctor said, "Twins," and for the first time I felt a small burgeoning of excitement. "Twin girls," I told myself. "I'm sure I'll have a nervous breakdown," I said. "Just think—twins."

And so I lie in the darkness at the end of another Mothers Day reflecting on my short seven and a half years of motherhood. Once again the red carnation passed out in Sunday School did not make it home intact; once again the Mothers Day talks laid a burden of guilt squarely on my shoulders. I know I don't deserve the Emma Riggs McKay Award for saintliness, but motherhood did not come naturally to me, and it still isn't something I revel in. Some people have a talent for childraising, just as some have a talent for English literature or selling real estate. The ones with talent for motherhood should have the large families.

Yet amid all the guilt and failure, there is an element,

elusively defined but tangibly felt, that keeps me going. Over the years a rhythm had come to my life, a rhythm tending to blur the edges of daily frustration, developing, I suspect, not from resignation to my lot, but from the ebb and flow of family love, the reality of which I could never have guessed in my working days. I have seen my second son solemnly handing me one of his treasured valentines to comfort me when I cried, my third son saying with a dimpled smile, "Thanks, Mom" for the cut-up orange I handed him; my firstborn bringing home an "A" report card; multitudes of unexpected kisses, neck-cracking hugs, chores sometimes done without the asking; family home evenings that sometimes come off; even a three-year-old thanking the Lord for his laundry bag. And one night my seven-year-old saying, "You have sweet dreams, too, Mom."

I guess it is not enough to say I wasn't prepared for this job. It seems a shame that we have to learn to grow and give, develop patience, kindness and forebearance by practicing on small human beings. But I do know this: Because of my children, I am a better human being today than I was ten years ago.

And tonight I feel the new babies within me tugging and pulling for their own private place in the universe, feeling also the first insistent cramps of labor. I look at the sweetly sleeping form of my husband with some pity, knowing that tonight he will not get the rest he's looked for all day. But tonight I am greedy for the life within me, for new babies to hold, new downy soft heads in which to bury my nose, tiny faces to kiss. They will drive me crazy, of course. They will also make my soul burst with pride and joy.

And I will love them.

Elinor G. Hyde

Tie a Knot and Hang On

"Don't open the bathroom door or you'll let the bird out," my friend called to her children, not seen, but definitely heard in the background, as we discussed over the telephone the status of her forthcoming book.

I could not resist asking why the bird was in the bathroom.

"Because the cat knocked over the cage, and if we don't keep the bird in the bathroom until we get the cage fixed, the cat will eat it." She was matter-of-fact in her reply, but she interrupted our conversation two more times without warning—once it was to tell one of her sons he'd just have to be patient until the gerbil decided to come out of hiding, or until Dad had time to sit up at night when it was quiet and try to catch it (the gerbil had been loose in a bedroom for three days)—and once more when she began to laugh at her twelve-year-old who was rolling on the floor in agony. (He had been defeated at some game by a much younger brother). I wondered how my friend had found time to write a book, a book not even about the trauma of raising a family! Obviously, her family motto was the same as ours: "Never a dull moment."

Many times I have surveyed my own house in dismay:

My fifteen-year-old son's new ten-speed bicycle parked just inside the kitchen door because it is replacing the one stolen from the carport and not recovered despite the best efforts of neighbor kids and law enforcement officials. Next to the bicycle are a large tool box, two bags of potatoes (each weighing fifty pounds and waiting to be carried downstairs to the storeroom), and two gym bags dropped over the heat vent just inside the front door.

That's the kitchen. In the living room are three basketballs, another gym bag and the pile of afternoon newspapers awaiting delivery to the neighborhood.

Childless couples just raise their eyebrows and ask, "Why does she allow such goings on?" Who knows? Because there is no way except allowing? Or because so much else is happening that these minor problems have become invisible?

After all, the water heater has sprung a leak, nearly all the appliances in the household need repairs, the battery on the car is temperamental, and more than likely a summons has just arrived on some teenage driver's forgotten parking tickets.

Or perhaps a mother is overwhelmed with the one hundred long-stemmed Tropicana roses on the kitchen table and other floral trimmings for a wedding. One hundred roses smell wonderful! So we ignore the inconvenience of preparing and serving dinner around them while one of our older daughters arranges bouquet after bouquet for the wedding of her friend next door. Why all this at our house and not in her own home-shop? Simple logic: it is more convenient to carry the gorgeous baskets, corsages and centerpieces next door than to transport them miles across town on a warm day. And to be truthful, we really don't mind. The beauty and joy created by this girl's talents at floral arranging more than repay any trouble or disruption.

There are days when the two-year-old mixes Karo syrup in the sack of oatmeal, smears toothpaste on the bathroom mirror, dumps perfume on his teenage sister's bed, and carefully drops plastic parts of a favorite game down a heat vent. While you are trying to clean it all up, you quietly discover he has also shut off the furnace and the water heater and you must call the gas company.

There are days when you discover that your older son has become this year's street bully. Only last year he was getting it and now he's giving it. No doubt his Eagle Scout application is returned that day with a wonderful note of congratulations to parents who have raised such an ideal son!

Do you laugh—or cry?

Recently I needed a large hank of rope for my Blazer scouts. I was expecting a few quizzical glances and stares as I waited at the checkout counter, and I had a clever answer ready. I was surprised though, when a little grandmother reached out, patted my arm and whispered, "That worked for me. When you come to the end of the rope, tie a knot and hang on. And when you've worn the knot thin, send for more rope." Her step was perky as she paused at the door and turned with a smile, "Good luck, dear."

We do it all by choice and nearly always cheerfully. Why? Because along with the bubblegum on the Sunday tablecloth and melted crayons in the clothes dryer, there are days when a small boy looks up at your bedraggled hairdo and says, "You're the bestest mother in the whole world."

Or you find a short note on your pillow the day after you've cooked two turkeys and helped prepare a formal dinner for seventy. The note says simply "Thanks, Mom." You know without asking that it is from the treasurer of the Pep Club Dropouts—(those girls who are super, but not showy). And you know she appreciates the time it took to shop and plan that formal dinner when the traditional restaurant banquet initiation seemed out of reach and you helped with the budget juggling and said, "If we did it ourselves we could . . ." You did, and the thank-you note means more than all the honors you could ever receive for outstanding achievement. Your daughter looked good to her friends that day.

Days like these sometimes may be few and far between, but only one makes it all worthwhile.

No one can tell a young bride-to-be what she is in for nor would she believe it if you tried. *She* will not live as you have. *She* will be *organized.* She has heard only sadness in your voice as you recall the time the bank account ran out just as the in-laws came from out of town for a lengthy visit. Until she does it herself she won't understand the triumph in those "original" meals of split peas over crackers and wheat casseroles you served without admitting to poverty.

Nor will she understand what it takes to keep a marriage happy until she survives her first major disaster. If she's lucky, that is the day he will spend his lunch money on violets. But violets or no violets, a woman is fulfilled in helping others. No better framework exists to meet that need than that of wife and mother.

So what if the seven-egg quiche the kids made runs out onto the oven and makes the house smell like burnt dog fur? What if her birthday gift is the sink unplugged, or her Christmas present is a new pair of Playtex rubber gloves to cover the exzema from diapers and dishes? Nothing the world offers in paychecks or glory can compare with the feeling of seeing each child tucked in bed, safe and secure.

Sure, tomorrow's another day—and your heart is likely to get crumpled. But these are God's children, lent to you for a few short years. You're going to give it all you've got. If there happens to be a thank-you afterwards, it is superfluous although appreciated.

After all, you owe it to your mother, don't you, to see that her grandchildren are raised right?

And you owe it to your children, as well. Wouldn't it be sad to have a mother who was a failure?

But most of all, you do it just because you are a woman who isn't about to quit until the job is done.

Edna B. Laney

The Last Project

In our many years together Bert and I faced many trials, but working together, we managed to bring to successful conclusion all the projects that come with a good marriage. We had raised seven children while budgeting for college and missions. (Our sixth missionary was in the field, our sixth college student was at BYU.) We had made the gospel a vital and important part of our lives, had endeavored to be active in the community and to spread the light of Christ wherever we were. Because Bert was a statistician, each project had been carefully planned and executed as near to the plan as possible. But now we would need all the faith and courage we could muster for our final project. As he leaned against the pillows and smiled at me, I returned his smile. Though I was filled with terror at the thought of life without him, I knew his need for comfort was greater than mine, and so my chin never even quivered.

With paper and pencil he began the planning. It was a familiar routine. He tried to cover all possibilities, to plan for every contingency. His first impulse had been to keep his condition a secret, but that would mean evasions, even outright lies. After some thought, we decided it would be easier for us to tell the truth. So we sat close together and worked on the plans for what he came to call, "Our honeymoon in reverse." Instead of knitting our lives together, we would now begin to unwind the strands and go our separate ways. My smile grew stiff, but his pencil never wavered.

"I've been trying to show people how a Latter-day Saint lives. Now I will show them how one dies," he said. I went to my next door neighbor and asked her to tell the other neighbors. I called the other children; I wrote to our missionary son as we informed the bishop and special friends.

We both agreed that the hospital, with its emphasis on life at any cost, with its needles, tubes and machines, would only prolong his suffering. I shuddered at the thought that I could be prevented from sharing his final moments by some well meaning doctor or nurse. So with our own doctor's approval, we made plans to keep him at home. Bert worried about the problems I might face, but I was able to convince him that I was strong enough to stand the stress. Besides, we belonged to a ward full of loving hands eager to do anything for us.

In the days that followed, we made many decisions. We made our wills. He wished to be buried in his home town of St. George, Utah, so we went to the mortuary to make funeral arrangements. He selected pall bearers and the speakers for the program; then he went on leave from his office and resigned other official duties. He cleaned out drawers and files. I bought his burial clothes and read countless books on death, dying and the problems of widowhood. We were still working our shift at the temple, though, because he wanted to continue as long as he could. In the meantime, we tried to make life as normal as possible.

During all this time Bert never said, "Why me?" He seemed to be entirely willing for God's will to be done. In his methodical fashion he made himself ready for what was to come. He never ceased to thank the Lord for his blessings and to ask for help and strength.

As Christmas neared, we prepared for the holidays partly by reciting a riddle: "What do you give a man for Christmas when he is dying?" We both thought about this for awhile. Bert's answer: "Vanishing Cream." I bought him an SX-70 camera (no waiting to develop the pictures) and then, after much thought, I gave him scriptures on tape. It would make it easier for him when he became too weak to hold a book.

Our many long talks brought us closer in mind and purpose than we had ever been before. We told each other things that in the ordinary course of life we might never have said. Each day was filled with special purpose. Each hour, each act had vital meaning. Each evening I said, "Will you be here tomorrow?" and he replied, "I think so." Each morning one of us would remark, "Well we have another day together."

Strangely enough, we were not depressed. Our home was a place of faith, hope, love and even laughter. Once, when I brought in an armload of his clean shirts, he looked at them and said, "Golly, that's enough shirts to last me the rest of my life." When he realized what he had said, we both managed to laugh.

One of the intimate customs of our married life was my habit of grabbing Bert hard and proclaiming dramatically, "You are my prisoner, and you cannot get away." One day when I playfully pinned his poor bony shoulders to the bed, he gave me a sly wink, and said, "Oh, yes I can." Once when we were wrangling, amiably, over something I had proposed to do, he said, laughing, "Over my dead body." I burst into tears.

While discussing arrangements for the funeral, he asked

me if I thought I should leave for St. George the same day and bury him the next. I said I thought we had better stay over a day because we would all be dead by the time we got there. "Like me?" he asked.

Some of my friends counseled me. "Never let him see you cry," but I wanted him to know I cared deeply, so I watered his chest nearly every day until the withdrawal stage. Then I tried not to intrude on his thoughts which were no longer of me or of this world.

Christmas came and most of the children were home. It was a happy time, with a great thread of sadness through everything we did. Bert joined us as much as he could. He would be up for a few moments and then would retreat to his bed, only to come out again a few minutes later. We tried to keep everything the same: the Christmas Eve program, the big Christmas dinner (with three desserts) and the visits from friends.

Bert took the opportunity to have a private interview with each child, giving each a father's blessing recorded on tape. He also made a tape for each of the absent boys. One evening he had interviews with the grandchildren, beginning with the oldest teen age girl and moving down to the youngest—a year old—boy. To those old enough to understand, he talked about death. He told them that he had been called to work for the Lord on the other side of the veil. Assuring them of his continued love, he promised that wherever he was he would think of them and look out for their welfare. The tiny ones were given last hugs and kisses from the grandfather they would one day be unable to remember.

Soon it was time for the children to go. Words cannot describe the feelings of each as final kisses were given, hugs, loving words, a last reluctant closing of the door.

Bert braced himself in the bay window as each car with its precious cargo faded from sight. One last wave and he went off to bed. From then on we were alone.

It soon became apparent that Bert would have to train his replacement at the temple. The day he cleaned out his locker and took "indefinite leave," we walked out arm in arm. "It is the end of an era," I said. He looked straight ahead, too overcome to speak. We sat a moment in the car looking at the temple through the windshield. Then slowly, wearily, he put the car in motion. It was the last time he would drive a car.

When President Eames came to the house to present a certificate of release from the temple, Bert held the paper in his hands and stared at it, an omen he could not ignore. "The time is getting close," he said. "When you are released from one position, they do not wait long to give you a new assignment." From then on he would frequently say, "I wonder what my new assignment will be," or "I wonder where they will send me." One day he said, "Would you be frightened if you woke up some morning and found me dead?" I said "Of course not." I hadn't been resting much before; now it became almost impossible to close my eyes.

Each day he grew thinner and weaker, but he fought to live. He spent much time trying to force down food. He would take a bite and tell me how bad he felt that he could not eat it. We had made a pact that we would try not to keep things from each other. Now we broke the agreement. I failed to tell him that the dryer was out of order. He tried to convince me that he was not hungry and was feeling only mild discomfort.

About this time friends began to bring messages for loved ones on the other side. He would listen carefully to each message, promising that if he saw the deceased ones, he would surely remember to tell them what was said. And then he worried that he might not be able to remember all the messages. I encouraged him by assuring him that he was still mentally competent.

Many friends who came to console left inspired and uplifted. Still we had our dark moments and times of despair. We were praying each day for his release. Death became our all consuming wish. It hurt so to see him suffer, but he never complained. To me he would admit to having "discomfort," but to those who came to see him he was always, "Just fine."

Since our doctor was in Baltimore, I suggested that he make out the death certificate in advance and send it to me. I would fill in the day and hour. When the certificate came, Bert spent quite a long time reading it. He said, "Not many men get to read their own death certificate." He asked for a mirror to study his skeleton face. I agreed that I would not care to meet such a face, suddenly, some dark night. He named himself "Boneypart." I could now put my thumb and middle finger about his wrist.

Bert was still in charge though he refused to let me get a nurse. He struggled to the bathroom; he forced himself into the tub each day. He said it made him feel better. I did him the courtesy of allowing him to do whatever he wished. With my help he managed to care for himself until the day before he died.

He often said how glad he was that he was home and not in the hospital. He would call me the best nurse in the world, and would add, "I hate to be a nuisance," or "You must be getting tired of taking care of me." When he finally offered to go to the hospital, I assured him that I would rest when his time had come. When I reminded him that this was our last project and that we would see it through together, he sighed with relief.

I do not pretend it was not hard, but there was a spirit in our home that brought confidence and peace to our hearts. He talked about his parents and expressed a wish that he might be "home" for his birthday, the first of March. I could see he was moving away from me emotionally just when I needed comfort more than ever. His mind was fixed on the world to come. He had reached the withdrawal stage. Because of what I had read, I understood it, but in many ways found it the hardest to bear.

Finally, he was in so much pain that I was giving him shots of morphine every few hours, and he was now too weak to lift his head from the pillow. I bathed him and changed the sheets. I cut the neck of a white shirt and put it on him. It made a passable bed gown. I had removed his garments and put away his slippers. We both knew he would not be out of bed again. When I finished, I leaned over and kissed him. "We haven't far to go now," I said. "It is almost finished."

"I'm ready," he replied. He stared at the ceiling and then at the clock.

"What are you looking for?" I asked. He did not reply. I knew he was watching for someone to come for him. Finally he seemed to sleep.

It was evening again as I sat in the living room talking to my stake president. The couch faced the stairs and hall. A dim light filtered out of the bedroom. Suddenly I saw the hall fill with forms. One of them beckoned to me. I excused myself and went up the stairs. The hall and bedroom were filled with forms who moved aside as I neared the bed.

Bert was gasping, his eyes closed. I took his hand. I thought of the others downstairs but decided that this was a moment for just Bert and me and those almost unseen guests who were there to welcome him. He struggled for breath. Twice he seemed to stop breathing but then resumed his pitiful wheezing. When I heard a rattle, a gurgle in his throat, I knew what it was. I had read about it in books. Dry eyed, I held his hand while he breathed his last, feeling triumph that we had successfully completed our last project together.

I said, "You are dead now, Honey. You've made it." I stood for what seemed a long time and talked to him, sure that he could hear all I said and all that I thought. Then I went to tell my guests that he would be home for his birthday.

His agony was over, but mine would continue. Now I began to understand why old people often die soon after a companion is taken. I see why it is possible for some who lack a firm faith to do away with themselves. But I struggle to remain filled with faith. I try to see that his cruel death had special meaning and purpose for us both.

Bert and I made plans for my life without him. He wanted me to finish college and do the traveling I loved. He set standards of faith and bravery that I find hard to reach. Now, as I study and travel and continue my work in the temple, I strive to fill my life with interesting projects. I try to think of ways to help others. There is so much I have learned; there is so much more I must learn. With Bert's example before me and the gospel to guide me, I cannot fail.

"Words always come after the fact.
Tse Her doesn't know the real words.
I don't know them either.
Some kinds of knowing
require no alphabet."
Donna Toland Smart

Rubina Rivers Forester

Mormon Brown

One Sunday as I sat in Sacrament Meeting in a Laie, Hawaii ward chapel, I noticed that Polynesian hands had carefully placed six vases, three of them foil covered cans, on the piano, pulpit, and organ. The "flowers" were multi-colored feathers in bright improbable combinations of forest green, white psychedelic orange, brilliant purple, bright blue, shocking pink, gold, maroon and chocolate brown. I could see that they were garish, and totally inappropriate for a place of worship, but I waited (I admit impatiently), till after the meeting when I overheard the comments I was expecting: "Now didn't you love those darling feather flowers?" "These Polynesians have a primitive sense of color, don't they?" "We're so lucky to be living among such happy, simple, people," "We'd never get away with that in Salt Lake City."

Being Mormon and brown is a straw that has sometimes strained my half-Samoan back. I suppose it is because in Hawaii our multi-ethnicity causes the weekly speakers to saturate their sermons with "We're all children of God," "We're equal in God's Church," "In God's eyes we're all the same color" (white, of course). The sermonettes spill out God's Word in easy-to-swallow pills—

pills to cure the infection of discrimination. Perhaps it is my fault that I haven't been cured, but I am still hurt when less is expected of me, when I am not allowed to discriminate also—beauty from tastelessness, quality from shoddiness, pride from selfishness.

A few years ago I was called to a position only because I could relate to the local people. I wish now that I had said something then. I may have been more attuned to my calling had I been chosen because I could relate to the Lord or to His teachings. It seems to me that the worth of my membership in the Church, the worth of my character and ideals are often based on my color. I'm judged and assessed by my skin pigmentation: "Why bother explaining. She won't understand," "Now how did she get the right answer?" "They can surprise you sometimes."

My children, on more than one occasion, have asked me, "What are we, Mom? Are we Samoans?" Frankly, the questions stump me every time. My children are 3/16th Samoan, 1/16th Chinese and 3/4th Caucasian. We're taught in the Church to search out our roots. I sometimes wonder if my children are not better off to forget about Hagoth and his great curiosity which started it all and concentrate on being what they look like—WASPS. I wish I could answer them with "We're Mormons." But though that answer may work in Hawaii where Mormons are inter-racial, it might sour on them in Utah where Mormons are inter-Caucasian.

I have analyzed my feelings on my nationality and cultural background and I can list them thusly:

I'm ashamed to be Samoan. (sometimes)

I'm ashamed to be Caucasian. (sometimes)

I'm proud to be Samoan. (sometimes)

> I'm proud to be Caucasian. (sometimes)
>
> I've always liked being Chinese because I don't look Chinese and so am free to pick and choose the best Chinese qualities.

I have yet to decide whether I am being complimented when a Relief Society sister declares, "But I don't think of you as a Samoan." I suppose that what I want to be is first Rubina, secondly Rubina, thirdly Rubina. It has nothing to do with egotism. I want the initial acceptance to be based on "name, rank, serial number" instead of "Who are you? Where do you come from?" Why not "What do you know, Rubina? I would like to know more."

Being half-caste produces many ambivalent feelings. When I touch an artistically painted, well-made piece of tapa cloth, I become reverent, proud, introspective. When I view the Samoan "taualuga" danced with lewdness and dishonor, I melt with shame and anger. When I write with English words a poem expressing joy in Polynesian things, I choke with gladness.

Missionaries fascinate me. Each year the Church sends thousands of them around the world. There, for two years they teach tolerance, for "other folds," about "gathering them from every nation, kindred, tongue, and people." When I arrived on the Provo campus from the Pacific twenty years ago, I expected the "Peaceable Kingdom" throughout the valley—a kingdom of lambs and many colors shepherded by returned missionaries. I met many missionaries who had served in my home country. They praised my mother's excellent cooking, the kindness of "the People," and raved about the "best two years of my life." Yet I nearly always felt a barrier, the "keep your distance," "east is east and west is west," the furtive look hoping a friend wasn't watching the encounter. I may as well have come from a leper colony on the moon for all the attention I got. I have concluded that a returned missionary's first step onto American soil is a small step into back-home discrimination and a giant step toward total forgetting. I have not forgotten. While it wounded me then with stabs of "Why? How could it be, Lord? He served two years among us. Why doesn't he understand?" now it just stings with, "We could have just been friends."

When I was a freshman and living in Heritage Halls, my roommates arranged blind dates for each other during the course of the year. No one ever arranged a blind date for me. I knew the reason. I was brown—brown different, brown unacceptable, a brown curiosity, brown "convert her but don't date her." In search for the essence of myself, I've played many roles—the Native Daughter Come Home, Miss Intellectual of Samoa, the Satisfied Single, the International Jetsetter, the Brilliant Wife Behind the Man, Saint Rubina, Super Mormon Mom, the Great White Half-Caste, and I've failed at them all. We Polynesians are often to blame for our lot in life. We good-naturedly accept the fawning, the condescension, toddler vocabulary, the ethnic jokes, the judgments made upon us. I know a former Relief Society president who, when she speaks with Polynesians, changes her language to pidgin English . . . and they, though they can speak English fluently and correctly, speak pidgin right back. I've seen many of my people through the years act at being "hula hula girls" and "swinging surfers" to provide local color and entertainment for the tourists and very often Church authorities.

I taught in Church schools in Samoa for six years; my husband worked for the Polynesian Cultural Center for the same number of years. Before a Church authority or dignitary arrives in either place, everything bustles. Cultural dances are learned, huts are re-thatched, drums are re-skinned, clothes are re-styled, new dialogues are memorized . . . suddenly it's "Bring out the natives." I have wanted to scream out more than once, "I'm not a museum piece!"

A year ago an angry Samoan sister, misunderstanding the inquiries I had made as Relief Society president, confronted me in my garage and while hurling accusations to my face, threatened to punch it. The words that pierced my heart with their sharpness all had to do with my pride (of all things) in being a big-shot Samoan.

"What am I?" haunts me, divides me, amuses me, frustrates me. It's like a Space Invaders game when you pit yourself against yourself. My educated half with the wider vision, the fuller understanding, the higher dreams pits itself against the Polynesian half with its quicker generosity, its plainer faith, its simpler needs. The conflict will be resolved (mathematical equasions do not lie). Two halves equal one whole.

The Mormon Church has rapidly become a worldwide Church in the past decade. If it is to survive its phenomenal growth it must teach its membership a whole-world thinking—a thinking that sparkles with acceptance, that warms with sensitivity and understanding, that glows with love for each special individual.

I now accept what I am—a unique child of God, a unique member of the Church. Perhaps this knowledge of myself, gained at the age of forty-one, will better prepare me to understand, to glean from, and to serve the international church of Jesus Christ.

Right after school began this past fall, my five-year-old came home with questions.

"Are we Catholics, Mom?"

"No, we're Mormons."
"Are we Hawaiians, Mom?"
"Yes, because we live in Hawaii."
"What color are we, Mom?"
"Sun-tanned."
"Mom, are we lucky?"
What do I answer?

Carol C. Ottesen

Reality and Imagination: Letter to a Friend

Dear Tom,

Though you are twenty-five years old and close to the paradigm of a carefree bachelor and I am twice your age, a wife, mother and grandmother, we are friends. Perhaps this is because being graduate school English majors together, we have been able to share some of our more profound ideas about how the world works. Through our association, we have built bridges that span the gaps in age, environment, values and beliefs, bridges made possible by our common human predicament.

Though you are obviously happy, gifted and well-adjusted, you have often expressed a vague discontent that seems to go beyond casual restlessness. Out of intellectual curiosity, you have asked me about my experience as a "thoroughly Mormon woman." You seem to see a paradox here between my intellectual life and the need for a suspension of logic in order to accept Mormon mystical foundations. You also question the Norman Vincent Peale happiness that arises from a certain immunity to reality which you see as at best a forced optimism. Is that my kind of happiness, you ask? If so, you say, it is not only hypocritical, but dishonest!

I was apprehensive when you consented to come to our home for Christmas. Besides five children and two in-laws, there were three grandchildren and assorted people invited out of the Christmas imperative to share. There were no cigarettes, drinks or country club service. When my husband called for prayer and everyone knelt, I knew you had had little experience with prayer, especially kneeling prayer.

Your visit included a trip to the church where my husband is a Bishop and I play the organ. Since you are a musician also you were inspired to ask, "Having a degree in music don't you find it painful to play for an untrained church choir?" When you found I wasn't paid, you seemed even more puzzled. Your question later was: Your life is so full of commitments. Don't you find it difficult to be so tied down to people and to rules?

I don't have all the answers, Tom, but I need to share with you some of the experiences I have had in pursuit of answers. I hope I do more than merely justify my position and that you can find some universal implications here. I will not be doctrinaire; I merely want you to understand in part how I feel about my family, my religion and my life.

As would-be writers, we have talked of realism, both interested in describing life "as it really is." Each of us reflects a personal conception of reality. I agree with poet Wallace Stevens when he says that reality is not enough; that to achieve "nobility," the poet must add the ingredient of imagination, or in other words, report the world "as it *can* be." Then Stevens says, the poet must set out to make this "imagination become light in the minds of others." The poet's role is "to help people live their lives."[1] He fails if he does not "give to life the supreme fictions without which we are unable to conceive of it."[2]

When I read Stevens, it struck me that his criteria for the making of a noble poem could also be applied to the making of a noble life. Both must be grounded in reality but must also add the imagination and vision that affirm reasons for being and lend an ecstatic freedom of mind.

After reading Stevens, I remembered a time long ago when I was still scabby knees and Shirley Temple curls standing with my father on a wind-swept day at Union Station in Washington, D.C. He looked up at the stone arch over the entrance to the station and read aloud the inscription engraved in gold on the facade: ''Where there is no vision, the people perish.''[3] His big, bony hand gave mine a little more pressure. ''I want you to remember that forever. Just as those words are engraved in that stone, engrave them in your mind.'' He repeated the inscription and asked me to repeat it back. The light changed and we moved on.

Dinner time at our house was a variation on this theme. My father was in the habit of pausing before prayer every evening to relate a particular experience of the day and to endow it with a larger meaning. I don't remember his being didactic; the effect was pleasant. That the ordinary could be made extraordinary lent a kind of order to chaos. I think all eight of us could detect even then that this was *his* way of survival as he led us through peeling potatoes and shining Sunday shoes on a magic carpet that out-distanced Tom Sawyer's fence painting ingenuity. This conditioning has made me especially receptive to an Emerson quotation:

> The invariable mark of wisdom is to see the miraculous in the common. What is a day? What is a year? What is a child? To our blindness these things seem unaffecting. When . . . we behold the higher

> law . . . so shall we come to look at the world with new eyes. Nature is not fixed, but fluid. Spirit alters, moulds, makes it.[4]

The difficulty comes in initiating this vision, this forming. First of all, none of us wishes to be thought of as naive, as "out of touch with reality," or after Quixotic windmills. Also, when commitments are made, there is the problem of life being so crowded with immediate concerns that seeing beyond them is difficult.

I remember the almost oppressive realization upon bringing my first baby home from the hospital that his life was in my hands, that I was now responsible for another human being. I thought how strange that having a baby was much better than I ever dreamed but also much worse than I ever anticipated. Five more children followed closely. The reality of confinement and fatigue made imagination and vision difficult. Diapers were forever; hearts and flowers were a thing of the past; I would never live long enough to go back to graduate school. Even reading was difficult after the children were in bed when my desire was subsumed by exhaustion. At these times imagination was hard to come by. I wish I had read Northrup Frye:

> Human intelligence can resist routine by arresting it in an act of consciousness, but the normal tendency of routine is to work against consciousness. The revolution of consciousness against routine is the starting point of all mental activity, and the center of mental activity is *imagination,* the power of transforming "reality" into *awareness* of reality.[5]

This awareness is where a poem and life as a poem begin.

Subsequently, I have learned at least three things which

I think I knew before but which had to be experienced. The first is that the writer of Ecclesiastes was right; there is a time and season for all things. The nesting/growing season is surprisingly short, in retrospect, and can be followed by a succession of springs.

The second is that just as writing a poem is ultimately an individual enterprise, so is the obtaining of vision and imagination. In the novel, *The Secret Garden* when Mary sees the invalid Colin walk for the first time, she says, "It's magic." "Yes," Colin answers, "the kind of magic you make yourself. And that is the best kind."[6] I see this not as naive optimism but as intelligent awareness of possibilities. Yeats writes of this magic, Emerson speaks of it as "new eyes," Stevens calls it imagination, God calls it vision.

The third thing I have learned is that synaptic moments occur often enough to re-charge life with light-giving electricity. The meaning and vision lent to these moments act as a sustaining power so that a continuum of happiness is possible.

Let me tell you, specifically, about some of these moments in my life. Some of them are quietly transcendent moments like the night I found a note under my pillow from my eight-year-old daughter who was disappointed when she didn't get a horse for her birthday. "Dear Mom," it read, "I love you more than a horse. Love, Your Gril, Lisa."

Some are more oceanic, like the incomparable experience of becoming a mother for the first time. When our first baby came, we had only been a few weeks in Los Angeles where my husband was to attend dental school. We had no relatives, no friends as yet and our landlady spoke only Spanish. When it became obvious that the baby was about to be born, my husband ran two miles in the middle of the night to find a public phone to call the doctor. When he came back and saw me, alone and afraid, he asked me if I would like a blessing. When he laid his hands on my head and blessed me, the spiritual bonding was not only an epiphanal experience but it lent me incomparable assurance. The next day, after a difficult birth, he came to see me, carrying a bunch of slightly wilted daisies. The occasion must be important, I thought, because he was wearing a suit, a convention he detested at the time. As he walked towards me, I noticed that in his excitement he had put on different colored socks. Bending over the bed and kissing me, he said, "Thank you for giving me a son!"

Nine months later as we sat in the back of a black limousine, our hands clasped over a small, white coffin on our laps, I was more than ever grateful for a philosophy of life that includes belief in the continuation of life. We know that we will be able to associate with this small son again. This is part of the religious form I have chosen for my life, just as a form is chosen for a poem. I like this quote from Cassirer: "Form finds truth—here is the whole." By living within this form, I am finding truths that work for me. Life seems to go better, just as does the writing of a poem, when there is a ruling metaphor, a unifying theme and a commitment to form.

Part of this chosen structure included the bearing of more children, as well as the incorporating into our family of five American Indian foster children. The last moment I would like to tell you about, took place with these children, (including an Indian daughter), ranging in age from 18 to 9 years old. It was September 5th, our wedding anniversary. The children blindfolded my husband and me and took us in separate cars to a nearby park. When they took off the blindfolds, we were seated at a table for two, candle-lit and beautifully set with china, silver and flowers. Although the cheese appetizers were a little stale, the Seven-Up slightly flat and the entertainment non-professional, they sang songs and told family jokes while standing on a platform in front of our table. The last song was "Edelweiss," our family song, accompanied by our nine-year-old on her squeaky violin. My husband and I joined in on the final "bless my homeland forever." Knowing that this might be our last time together for a long while, we found it difficult to keep back the tears. After the children ran down to us from the platform, we became for a few moments a solid lump of hugging humanity. Simultaneously happy and sad, looking both backward and forward, we felt that one little corner had been cleared in the earthy process of "seeing through a glass darkly." Life is seldom perfect, but moments like these *are.*

Viewed in its totality, family life has the potential of providing peak experiences not available in any other social situation, as well as potential for being the world's most efficient support system. It's hard to imagine not coming home from the impersonality sometimes pervasive in graduate seminars to a place of non-judgmental acceptance and perfect ease.

Yet, I acknowledge, as does T. S. Eliot, that between the ideal and the reality "lies the shadow." The pain of commitment to people or to institutions is real; the ideal is not often reached; human relationships bog down. Acknowledgement of the gap between the reality and the ideal is the first step in dealing with that shadow. The next is making a conscious choice not to fall into the shadows where cynicism or "quiet desperation" block the vision of hope for the ideal. This requires great patience with people, institutions and self as each struggles to make the ideal a reality. I am reminded of Whitman's noiseless, patient spider who stood on a promontory isolated, launching forth filament out of itself. "And you, O my soul, where you stand," Whitman says, "Surrounded, detached in measureless oceans of space/ . . . venturing, throwing, seeking the spheres to connect them/ Till the bridge you will need be form'd . . ./ Till the gossamer thread you fling catch somewhere/ O my soul."[7]

One of the implications here seems to be the continual venturing, spinning and launching forth. I have just made a trip to Utah for my father's eightieth birthday where he is one of the souls still venturing forth, though he is no longer the articulate college professor and church leader of the past. At age 77, when he had been home only a week from a church diplomatic mission to the Middle East, he suffered a severe stroke that rendered him speechless and paralyzed the right side of his body. At the present time he is in a wheelchair in full possession of his mind but able to say only a few limited words—literally a mind trapped in a body. His wife, an active woman of 62, is entirely responsible for his care. When I came home to Provo to see them, I didn't know what to expect—sadness, a little bitterness maybe, surely depression. When I arrived about 9:00 in the morning my mother answered the door, groomed and dressed for the day. She explained she was just dressing my father, that they'd be out in a minute. She wheeled him out a little later, fully dressed and as dapper as if he were just leaving for an appointment. Our cheeks met; there were tears as he struggled to say my name, laughing at his struggle and laughing again because he was crying. He continued to try to talk, laughing at his mistakes and a little impatient at my not understanding him. Later, he beat me at chinese checkers with great zest. When it came time to write in his journal, he wrote painstakingly for over an hour with his left hand to produce just one paragraph in simple sentences. When guests arrived for lunch, Mother wheeled him to the table, put a towel on him for a bib, wiping the saliva from his mouth occasionally during the meal, matter-of-factly without embarrassment to either of them. When it was time for his walk into the living room, I observed how much they seemed to be enjoying one another, this tiny woman supporting and steadying this large man. The task seemed not unpleasant just a simple exchange of love and caring that transcended duty. He playfully pulled her close after she re-seated him in the chair. ''Good,'' he said. She laughed and turned to me. ''You know, this is a beautiful time in our lives. He has cared for me all these years, and now I am able to care for him. We've never known such closeness. I suppose this is because I must read his thoughts and say his words. Yes, this is a beautiful time.'' She was not just repressing negative feelings or ''thinking positive.'' Their happiness was without affectation. Somehow, too, the satisfaction their life accomplishments have brought seems to have prepared them to accept their present limitations.

Do you remember our discussion of a poem of mine when you pointed out several words which were not only non-functional but didn't contribute to the unity or tone of the poem? Essentially, eliminating the non-functional is what my parents seem to have done with their lives. No one could blame them for being cynical, but bitterness or withdrawal do not fit the form they have chosen. All actions point toward the ruling metaphor. The product is functional, aesthetic and a model for others—their lives beginning to be a work of art.

I remember again my father's insistence on my repeating as a child, ''Where there is no vision, the people perish." Yet I also remember a very real wooden paddle called "The Reminder" that he put in contact with my backside several times to bring me back to reality. I believe that this consciousness of reality blended with vision or imagination has transformed this last phase of life into his finest hour. Yet, at times, I see on his face a pain that seems to come from a realization of the disparity between reality and the ideal. Paradox and irony never reach total resolution. My father and I are consoled that we are not alone in this struggle, that life's paradoxes can be seen as incentive to continue venturing forth for a view from the promontory where reality is only a type or symbol of the greater, more perfect life.

Much more is begging to be said. This is only a beginning. How about coming to our house next Christmas? I promise you a meal that's a work of art, but just to keep you in touch with reality, you may wash the dishes.

Lovingly,
Carol

---

[1]Wallace Stevens, *The Necessary Angel,* (New York: Random House, 1951), p. 20.

[2]*Ibid.,* p. 31.

[3]Old Testament Proverbs, Chapter 29:18.

[4]Ralph Waldo Emerson, *Selected Writings,* "Nature," (New York: Random House, 1940), p. 41.

[5]Northrop Frye, *Fables of Identity, Studies in Poetic Mythology,* (New York, London: Harcourt, Brace, Jovanovich, 1963), p. 239.

[6]Frances Hodgson Burnett, *The Secret Garden,* (Philadelphia: Lippincott, 1938), p. 202.

[7]Walt Whitman, *The Portable Whitman,* "A Noiseless Patient Spider," (New York: Viking Press, Inc., 1974), p. 254.

Ann Edwards-Cannon

In Celebration of Female Friends

There I was—twenty miles outside of Salzburg and instead of frisking joyously about the hills with a guitar and bellowing "Edelweiss" at the top of my lungs, I was immured in the tiny gasthaus where our BYU semester abroad group was staying.

My contact lenses had ungraciously popped out of my eyes on a train somewhere between Zurich and Innsbruck the night before, and I was so blind that I couldn't even see the Alps sprouting like weeds across the street. My roommate Donna kept assuring me the mountains were there in all their Tryolean splendor, and I believed her—I just couldn't see them. Needless to say, sightseeing at that point sounded like a dreary idea, so in my best "I'll-just-sit-here-and-suffer-while-you-go-out-and-have-a-good-time" voice I told Donna to go into town without me. Instead, she went straight to the little grocery store across the street (the one standing right next to the Alps) and bought enough cookies and Coca-colas to last the day. When she returned, we wrapped huge down quilts around our shoulders, sat by the tiny window, and said pithy things about other people.

It was wonderful.

Later that afternoon, one of the group's few males, Steve, poked his head through our doorway, presumably to see how we were getting along. Instead of speaking, however, he just stood there with a funny grin on his face and left. Moments later he returned with his roommates, Rod and Greg. They too stared at us for a moment before disappearing.

Over dinner that evening I asked Rod just what the three of them had found so interesting. "Oh, nothing."

"Come on," I said, "you obviously dropped by to see something."

He laughed—a little sheepishly I thought. "Okay. We came to see you and Donna."

I was thoroughly confused. It certainly was not as though they'd never seen us before.

Rod explained himself. "Steve told us to follow him if we wanted to see something neat. When we saw you two enjoying one another's company so much, we knew what he meant." Then he added, "To tell you the truth, I think we were all a little jealous."

That experience has stayed with me, reminding me always that the relationships I have had with women from the time I was young have been extremely important to me. I *need* my women friends. I do not function well without them. Unless I have at least one or two women in the circle of people close to me at a given moment, I am sunk. Period.

Given this fact, I have wondered why I find close female friends so necessary. I remember an essay I once read about the phenomenon of female friendship by a feminist who claimed that women automatically *bond* (I just love that word) because of their biological similarities, a notion suggesting that if two people have four breasts between them, they'll get along just dandy. I find the premise absurd, one that gives the old dictum "biology is destiny" new dimensions of perversity.

Yet, I do seem to require strong working relationships with other women. In the final analysis, my reasons are simply and strictly my own.

I need other women to laugh with. It is uncanny, but if another woman and I can smile at the same things, regardless of personality differences, I can guarantee we will be friends. It is not that I don't find men funny or that I cannot laugh with them as long and loudly as I laugh with women—it's just that I find something incredibly comfortable and warm about sharing laughter with a person of my own sex.

Perhaps I feel this way because I've always had the good fortune to associate with funny women, beginning with Cindy in the sixth grade. Cindy got her kicks from such varied activities as spitting out cherry pits at speeding cars and borrowing eggs at midnight from surly neighbors. Although her antics could properly be called obnoxious, they did reveal a certain wit in an eleven-year-old girl. Cindy was constantly possessed by urges to accomplish the outrageous: one day as we played *Life* in her bedroom, she suddenly stood up and jumped out of her second-story window—just to see what it felt like. Cindy landed squarely on her mother's lone tomato plant.

It was because of Gigi that I survived home economics. When we were in the eighth grade, we were informed that for the future of our families and the United States of America, we had to take home economics. It didn't matter in the least that both of us intended to join the Peace Corps upon graduating, we had to learn how to put a zipper in an

A-line skirt and make pizza dough out of Basic Mix; we had to color-key ourselves with material swatches and make Simple Simon Fudge at Christmas time; we had to analyze our wardrobes and set a table for a formal dinner. We had to do all these things even though all either of us wanted to do was escape to some underprivileged country and grow wheat. So Gigi and I griped and griped and griped some more at the perversity of an educational system that forced Betty Crockerhood on two unwilling souls just because they happened to be female. Yet, for all our complaining, Gigi and I helped one another learn some simple skills and both of us remember the entire experience with surprising fondness.

While women are wonderful to laugh with, they are essential for swapping gripes. I need good women friends who can emphathize about those things that irritate me—things that a man, no matter how sympathetic, can never understand. I need someone who has actually attended Relief Society to truly understand how I feel about such things as wall-to-wall visual aids at stake preparation meetings, ferns on lacy tablecloths for Spiritual Living lessons, and the automatic assumption that Relief Society sisters are simply dying to stage yet another ward dinner.

I need my women friends for their enthusiasms. Because of Lisa I discovered Tillie Olsen and her short story of rare power "Tell Me a Riddle." Because of Laurie, who has seen *The Rose* at least a dozen times by now, I appreciate the bizarre magic of Bette Midler who says things like "What I want to know is where Her Majesty gets those *hats*." Because of Connie and Jerri and Nancy, I can feebly trek cross-country on skis. And because of Patrice I was once a member of the Provo City swimming team for an entire week.

Perhaps all of these things—laughing, griping, learning—ought to be placed into the larger context of shared experiences. Though roles and expectations of both sexes are rapidly changing, the fact remains that those events, frustrations, and concerns experienced primarily by women can best be understood by another woman. This natural empathy, in turn, can and very often does lead to systems of mutual support. I count it as a great blessing that I have one friend I have known practically all of my life; together we have supported one another in our quests to master the business of living.

Becky and I have known one another since grade school. From the first our friendship was characterized by long conversations—about family members, friends, school, future plans, dreams, and most important, feelings. Becky and I have always been able to share our feelings honestly with one another. One of the topics on which we have expressed ourselves with great vigor is the Church and our role in it. The feelings we have explored range from frustration to devotion.

The frustration stems from our difficulty in reconciling our interests and the economic realities of today with what we (perhaps mistakenly) have perceived as the traditional role of women in the Church. When we were younger, our plans for the future extended immodestly beyond the home. When I was thirteen, becoming a rock star and seeing my face plastered across the cover of *Rolling Stone* sounded considerably more intriguing than standing hip deep in diapers. Yet there was little encouragement in primary and MIA to explore alternatives that did not immediately involve home and family. While the boys our age shot baskets in the gym, ran rapids in Canada, and raised money for summer trips to Disneyland, we girls sat demurely in class listening to lessons on chastity and temple marriage.

As Becky and I grew older and became friends as well as daughters to our mothers, we obtained a new perspective on homemaking and motherhood, one characterized chiefly by respect and admiration. At the same time both of us have worked our entire married lives, not necessarily out of desire but out of economic necessity. At this point I do not foresee a time when I will not be working outside the home at least part-time. This is in no way a commentary on my husband's willingness or ability to support a family; it is a commentary on the way our society is changing. In light of this, I cannot help but feel that the Church could do more than it is now doing to help women explore new responsibilities and opportunities.

If Becky and I have at times experienced frustrations because of our membership in the Church, we have also regarded it as a source of incredible joy. In particular, a shared belief in the notion that ties carefully wrought during this lifetime can continue into the next life has given our friendship a spiritual quality.

Not long ago I was very ill. Each day dawned gray with the possibility that things might never be the same for me again. Then one afternoon a friend from my grade school days appeared with gifts. And what magic gifts they were: Teresa had brought me books wrapped in red and silver—books written for children and by children, and together they reminded me of that wizardry of childhood, the belief that life is new and precious. They reminded me of that childlike optimism which says life can be taken and shaped into something fantastic and rare. It was as if Teresa knew how important her gifts would be to me as I struggled to recover.

My women friends have been there for the Big Moments—for the Field Day Awards, First Dates, Graduations, Weddings, and Babies. But their presence at the grand showy events of my life would not have mattered had they not been there first to share the quiet moments. The hours of swimming, skiing, horseback riding, watching television, going to rotten movies, having Christmas gifts, sending notes, comparing notes, hating Girls' P.E., camping out, and always, always talking together have made us vitally and forever aware of one another. If there is such a thing as female bonding, I believe it must be very much like the bonding which takes place between husband and wife, parent and child, brother and sister. It takes place over the days and the weeks and the years spent together. I need my women friends, yes, but I also value them for themselves. For their wealth of kindness and courage, their humor and tolerance, their talents and dreams, I celebrate them all.

Donna Toland Smart

Tse Her, My Sister

After all this time, I still find my feelings hard to articulate. Perhaps the reason is that words have never been part of our relationship. Our communication has been by intuition, emotion, instinct. That does not matter, of course, since words are only symbols for reality. Realizing this, I was intrigued to discover in the story of Mother Eve, a kind of metaphor for Tse Her. The passage is found in Genesis 3:6—

> And when the woman saw that the tree was good for food and that it was pleasant to the eyes, and a tree to be desired to make one wise, she took of the fruit thereof, and did eat, and gave also unto her husband with her; and he did eat.

The need to nourish, to be nourished and the need for beauty, the need to learn and to make use of learning, and the need to share with loved ones—woman's common umbilical cord, spans through the centuries backward as far as Eve.

Tse Her has never read Genesis because she cannot read, even Hmong. She cannot write her name, and the uncertain lines of her "X" reveal how painfully her hand shook as she signed the official documents required of refugees to this country. Eating apples is a challenge because her teeth are decayed to a point well below the gumline.

Tse Her. Proper pronounciation touches the *t* only lightly and puts the stress on the *se*: tSay Her. According to Hmong custom, she retains her maiden name although she is married to Cha Xeng Yang and has given birth to seven children. When she arrived in the United States, four of those children, all married, and five of her eleven grandchildren were still suffering the indignities of the Thai Refugee Camp that for five years spelled the lone and dreary world for Tse Her.

In January of 1980, through the Catholic Charities Resettlement Office, we invited Cha Xeng Yang, Tse Her, and their only unmarried son, Cha Yang, into our lives. I suppose we were trying to ease our feelings of guilt for having so much. Although we saw this as only a peripheral effort, we hoped to relieve some human distress. And how very distressed Tse Her and her family appeared when I met them at the Western Airlines Terminal! Cast out once more from familiar surroundings, she presented a forlorn and suffering sight.

Not the men, however. In that society as in ours, they seemed constrained to play the patriarchal part of courageous leader. When I met them, the father and son each delicately placed his hands together, smiled, and bowed slightly. Cha Yang even ventured, "Hello—?" the inflection rising at the end like a question. Since that moment they have never failed to exude containment, calm control, and self discipline.

It was not that Tse Her's demeanor showed lack of discipline. She simply was not playing her role according to script. Despite her obvious misery, she conveyed a womanly essence that filtered into my consciousness and was to perfume our relationship from then on. The top of her head, which barely reached my chin, was swathed in a traditional black cotton headwrap. Obviously awry, it perched ludicrously at an angle as strands of black hair straggled out around one ear and over the back of her neck. Although her papers showed her to be near my age (around fifty), wrinkle-free olive skin stretched taut and smooth over classically high cheekbones. And, oh, her eyes! Dark and brooding they were, and filled with mysterious glimmers of past and future.

The rest of her clothing consisted of a new, dark blue parka worn over a sky-blue polyester cardigan, an ankle length, black cotton wraparound skirt, splashed with flowers, and incredibly small white sneakers. From her arm dangled a black cotton handbag embroidered in geometric cross-stitching, hot pink and chartreuse tassels fringing the bottom.

First impressions. Today I wonder what she thought of me then. I wonder if she has since stared into my inner spaces, as I feel I have into hers—comprehending somewhat more of myself. I have with Tse Her experienced an intuitive sharing of secrets all women hold in common. Our commitment to Catholic Charities, however required sharing more than secrets. For some weeks we shared our home; for much longer, our resources of time and energy. The Yangs needed unflagging support in their adjustment to life in a strange land among strange people, with strange values and strange idols. We find they still do but with less frequency.

Everything appeared outlandish that day—to me, too. The terrifying escalator in the terminal, so bravely conquered by father and son, so carefully avoided, for her sake, by Tse Her and me. The automatic doors, so abruptly startling. The automobile and other mechanical marvels, so recklessly present on the hard-surfaced roads, so different from simple mountain trails. The soaring and abundant buildings, so overpowering. The massive white-washed mountains, so cold and confining. Elements of civilization and elements of nature so kaleidoscopic. And yesterday's snowstorm still on the streets, so foreign and fearsome. They had never seen snow. Tse Her did not even wish to feel the fragile flakes frost her skin, nor to witness the miracle of snow turned to water. There were too many miracles to fathom: electric lights, door knobs, locks, water taps, electric cooking units, washing machines, dish washers, beds, bathrooms, supermarkets. Learning flung itself at them from every angle. And the men reacted with a bravado born of necessity, it seemed. For Tse Her, instinct took precedence over necessity. "She's the preserver of the race," my husband said. "She must be cautious."

I discovered she was not just cautious. On some occasions she was adamant. We had been wisely advised by the Resettlement Office to allow our Asian family to choose, cook and eat their own food in order to postpone the adjustment to American eating habits. Although the Yang men sampled American food with gusto, and my husband honestly savored theirs, Tse Her, with a shy smile and a single, slight but definite shake of the head, declined. I understood. She did not wish to taste our ice cream, and I was not eager to sample her boiled fish heads. In time she learned not to fear the voice filtering through the holes of the telephone receiver, but she steadfastly refused any enjoinings to reply.

Of course, at first she was more than cautious; she was ill. Motion sickness had plagued her from the moment she left camp for her first bus ride to Bangkok, Thailand and again from the moment of liftoff in the jetliner until it taxied into Gate #3 in Salt Lake City. She accepted that infirmity matter-of-factly. Perhaps she had cultivated such a trait from the time of the Communist disruption of her pastoral life in Laos, through the routings from other dwellings in other places, during the surviving of five, squalor-filled years of thirst and hunger in a teeming refugee camp. In the automobile whenever she felt sick, she matter-of-factly took a folded plastic bag from her pocket, turned her head, quietly gagged into it, tied the top, and disposed of it. This ritual became commonplace whenever she went anywhere in a moving vehicle.

Despite our sympathy with their struggle to adapt, despite the pathos of their past experience, we did recognize some touching ironies in our mutual adjustment. For example, I decided after several weeks that Tse Her's stomach must be reconditioned. Before a very necessary errand by car, I offered her some pills for motion sickness, which she obediently swallowed, but with considerable difficulty. When we arrived at our destination, she had not yet needed her plastic bag. But she was so in the habit of doing so that she remained in the back seat attempting to heave into the opened bag.

Numerous incidents punctuated the differences between cultures. Some of them seem exaggerated enough to be the substance of slapstick comedy. In our home they were pathetic reminders of complacent materialism. Tse Her and her family tried to cook a fish directly on the stove top, without benefit of skillet or wok. The sticky rice that is their staple food almost sealed the blades of my disposal.

But they were eager to learn, and they never repeated a mistake. They showed a genuine interest in being helpful, as well. Tse Her polished the stainless steel sink to such a high gloss that to turn on the water tap was to desecrate it. After I had demonstrated how to dust, she eagerly and thoroughly dusted—even the overstuffed furniture and the carpets on the floors. They worked quickly at every task, polishing windows and pushing the vacuum cleaner like anxious children who believe that a speedy worker earns greater approval. By our standards very small matters gave them pleasure—or were cause for alarm. They sat entranced, almost hypnotized, before the television set as they enjoyed color, patterns and sound, despite their lack of comprehension. And yet, turning the knob to open a door or pulling one shut created difficulty for Tse Her. When, because of her failure to close it, the car door flew open as we rounded a corner—almost spilling her out—Tse Her endured what sounded like a severe tongue-lashing from her son. I presume at that moment experience gave birth to comprehension. She now lives in a society whose openings close with doors. Failure to close doors is dangerous.

Yes, Tse Her learned to close doors, but for me, she figuratively opened them. She gave me a fresh look in a different direction. Offering fumbling assistance with the Yang's transition, I became entangled in conflict: between necessity and sufficiency; between must and want; between rudiments and riches. With Tse Her I confronted the primary levels of my own life, and assessed my own values. I smile now as I recognize that what matters most are nourishment for self and loved ones of body and spirit, pleasant surroundings, and intellectual stimulation.

When Tse Her smiles, reluctantly, her lips shyly hide

her naked gums. But her smiles, I have noted, spread from lips to eyes to inner soul. Tse Her smiled, and I wept when she, seeing our grandchildren for the first time, gathered the smallest into her arms and cradled him as long as he would allow it. Months later when at our invitation her married son and daughter-in-law and their three children arrived from the dismal Thailand camp, she at once gathered those twin girl babies and the three-year-old boy into her arms and for the first time laughed aloud. For me, that laugh was timeless and universal. Since my own married daughter and her children had accompanied me to the airport and to the Yang's apartment, we could intimately experience and translate into our own lives this Yang mother-child-grandchildren reunion. Tse Her, I've said, exulting, laughed aloud. Her son, Ge Yang, and his wife, Vang Xiong, my daughter and I, simply allowed the silent tears to fall unabated down our cheeks. No words were spoken for long minutes. Then the fast flow of language between the reunited family members began.

Words always come after the fact. Tse Her doesn't even know the real words. I don't know them, either. Some kinds of knowing require no alphabet. Tse Her knows good and evil; the contrast between real physical hunger and full bellies; between psychological hunger in being separated from loved ones and a full larder.

She also knows, I sense, the heightened desire for beauty that comes with its absence. "The woman saw . . . that the tree was pleasant to the eyes . . ." the Bible tells us. Pleasant to the eyes pitifully understates the exquisite loveliness of the rectangle of cross-stitch embroidery Tse worked in that squalid camp and presented to me. Two months of eye-straining and finger-challenging labor are woven into this elegant piece of Hmong artwork. At the time of its creation she was living in a crude, open, one-room shack in the camp, cooking scant rations over coals, fighting frustration and boredom and fear, as well as disease and thirst and hunger. As I examine the tri-colored, hand-sewn borders with their tiny stitches and carefully mitered corners, I marvel at the quest of womankind for beauty, at her ability to create it in spite of bitter circumstances. Simply framed in order not to distract from its own intrinsic loveliness, this gift represents Tse Her's instinctive longing for beauty. It now hangs in my bedroom—a constant reminder.

Tse Her brought much more than her embroidery. She brought her own sense of propriety in relationships. We observed a vivid illustration of this when the Yangs invited us to celebrate with the other Hmongs their New Year celebration early in December. We found some empty chairs in a church cultural hall brimming over with at least six hundred refugees. We noted the native costume worn by many and turned our attention to the music and dancing and narration on stage. As soon as she could appropriately do so, Tse Her left her place by her family and threaded her way across the large hall to a chair beside mine. She smiled toothlessly, gave her characteristic little nod, reached for my hand and squeezed it. Side by side we sat, she as hostess, my husband and I as guests, with no need for words. She had assumed her proper role there (with a natural gracefulness, I might add), and we accepted ours—to adjust to their culture, to eat their food, to spend some time and energy in learning more of their friends, to see their pride and enjoyment in their native celebration. Joy and comradery mingled together in a great display of color and noisy humanity.

Tse Her and her family have joined the Mormon

Church. They now live in a small apartment with two sons, two daughters-in-law and five grandchildren, including a brand new baby. Even so, they are less crowded than in the Thailand camp. Another son and his two children live nearby. Happily, a daughter and son-in-law and more grandchildren are now settled in California, where Tse Her visited recently. The Yangs own a second-hand black and white television set, and a used but roomy car. Tse Her has made some small contribution to family finances by working as a dishwasher in a popular local restaurant. She can now ride the bus to work without her folded plastic bag. She will soon sport new dentures and a new smile. She answers the telephone eagerly; she recognizes my voice, and she usually understands.

I hope that as she learns the English words, her basic values will not change. I hope they will tenaciously cling to me and to her—Tse Her, my sister.

Phyllis Barber

Oh Say What is Truth?

1950. Childhood in southern Nevada.

> Eeney, meeney, miney, moe,
> Catch a nigger by the toe.
> If he hollers, make him pay
> Fifty dollars every day.

We laughed and divided into teams.

"Don't ever sit behind Peola Martin," I said. "She never takes a bath. None of them ever do."

"I dare you to go through Westside after dark," my friend said. "The jigs'll get you if you stop. They have these little shacks you see, and right next to these dumps, they park their big flashy Cadillacs with furry dice hanging from the rear view mirror and fur inside the back window."

I didn't need to ask why the Negroes didn't have the Priesthood. Why should they?

1960. High School. I stood at the edge, arms folded across my waist, watching bodies move to the music. Wishing I were one of those females with one of those males and moving to the music. My red taffeta rustled with every shift in weight, the red dress with a velvet bow at the neckline. Matching red shoes too. All for *Red Mill,* the school operetta.

Before the performance, one crew member had told me that red was my color, and I almost felt pretty that night. My foot tapped out the rhythm of the dance music. I longed to move.

"Would you like to dance?" someone asked.

"Oh yes," I said eagerly before I had time to think.

He led me out to the "dance floor"—really the stage. His right hand rested loosely on my waist, my left barely touched his shoulder. As our hands joined, I stared. There, in living color, was my white against his black. Black and white. Real black and white. Good/Evil. Lightness/Darkness. Clean/Dirty. All of the absolute opposites. All of a sudden I began to feel crawly, itchy. "Who's watching me?" Agitation, perspiration.

Not flashy, he turned and swayed to the slow music, guiding me through seeming swarms of cast members.

"You play the piano very well," he said.

"Oh thanks. You sing . . ." I stammered, realizing that because he was a member of the chorus, I had never heard his voice alone. "You sing, don't you?"

My hand was wet. Red circles under my arms blackened the redness of my dress. Everything was turning to black. I imagined my skin turning black on contact, the blackness absorbing into my tissues cell by cell.

"I like to sing," he said. "Mrs. Dodsworth is a good leader."

"She's terrific," I said, wanting to enjoy this perfectly acceptable person. This nice person. This gentle person. This black one.

"I'm afraid that I'm not feeling well." I said the words

before I could grab them back. "Please excuse me. I'd better go home."

I left him standing in the middle of the dance floor.

The warm spring air cooled my wet surfaces as I gunned the motor of the old Plymouth. The moon lapped up black edges of night all around, licking the hairline of the shadows. White moon/Black night.

1966. As a Relief Society counselor in a university ward, I heard the stake leaders announce that, once again, it was time for bazaars. We returned to our ward to inform the ladies that it was time to break out their sewing machines and their #9 needles to stitch a contribution to the Relief Society.

Our work director was married to a radical thinker, some said, but she was still my best friend.

"Why can't we," she asked at our planning meeting, "instead of spending hours on a useless decorative pillow, go into the community, especially the black community, and serve there. We could have a cultural exchange day, teach young girls some homemaking skills. They could teach us something too."

"But the stake has given us the bazaar assignment." The Relief Society president looked tight through the lips and eyes.

"But we've got to get outside of this close-knit little group and help other people," the work director insisted. "How can the Gospel be realized if we don't?"

"We don't instigate our own programs. We follow the direction of the General Board."

"But, we could do this in addition to our bazaar assignment. What do you think, Phyllis? You haven't said anything." They both turned to me.

I wanted to agree with my friend, the work director. I also did not want to cross the Relief Society president.

"I think you both have good points to make," I said, the diplomat avoiding the razor's edge. "Maybe we could talk about some activity with the minorities after the bazaar is over."

"But we can't keep putting these things off."

"I think Phyllis is right," said the president. "We'll talk about it after the bazaar. Let's delegate the assignments."

Trouble is, one bazaar turned into a luncheon which turned into a ward party. It just changed form—like a chameleon. Same body, different colors. Green, brown, beige, even orange, but no black. It wouldn't blend in.

1970. I went to say good-bye to her. My husband and I were moving from the San Francisco Bay Area to Salt Lake City. Maitland had been the live-in housekeeper while we had been the outback renters of the gardener's cottage on the same estate. For $20 a month utilities and services rendered, we had employed the gentleman's method of scrimping through law school.

"You goin' to live with all those Mormons?" she asked.

"I guess so, but I'm one too. Haven't I ever told you, Maitie?"

"No."

As the long-time maid in this wealthy and politically powerful household, she had learned to be circumspect. Knowing her as I did, I knew that her momentary silence weighed at least fifty pounds.

"How can you be a member of a church that feels that way about us?"

"I don't have any bad feelings about your people."

"Then you shouldn't belong to a group that doesn't accept us as equal."

"But that's not how it works, Maitie."

"Are you sure?"

We said our good-byes.

Growing up outside "Zion," I had been weaned on a slight bias: Utah Mormons didn't appreciate the Gospel; the breathing, pulsing Church operated in spite of the stagnant center place. Too much inbreeding. To much nonrecognition of the human condition. Too much taking things for granted.

With two tiny sons and a businessman/millionaire-or-bust husband, I drove into the smiling jaws of Salt Lake City sans Conestoga. My phone didn't ring. When I phoned out, everyone politely explained that they were busy with their children, husbands, mothers, grandmothers, aunts, cousins or nephews.

"What about the family of man? What about me?" I mumbled to myself. I had no relatives in this city.

The walls of our home moved in at least two inches daily. Spring was grey and late. Depressed, I read Dostoyevsky's *Crime and Punishment* to distract myself. It didn't home. When I was thirteen, becoming a rock star and seeing my face plastered across the cover of *Rolling Stone*sound-Main, I and two children under the age of three. The owner/matre'd/water ignored us. It took me one hour to get the message that he didn't serve women with children. No one said anything. It was all understood.

"Thanks a lot for ignoring us," I said and stomped out the door. Never having been discriminated against before,

I raged all the way to McDonalds. "Who does he think he is? What right does he have to do that to me—a human being? That little tin god."

Suddenly, I took a large, wide-eyed stare into my soul. Here I was, feeling discriminated against by Utah Mormons with only their immediate families in mind and by a restaurant owner who ignored mother/children combinations. How must black people have felt all these years? Maitie's question haunted me . . . "You wouldn't belong to a group that doesn't accept us as equal." For all of my insistence that I was non-prejudiced, maybe I, myself fell short.

Because blacks had been denied the Priesthood, I had operated from an underlying assumption—superiority. While my mouth spoke pretty words, I subtly relegated part of my human family to the background with my cushioned amenities, my unwillingness to hold ground for them. I said things like "Them. Those people." Distancing words. Smiles with a closed soul.

My lonely hours diffused into fragmentary visions of blackness, of being black, of feeling black, of realizing that a black skin hadn't always counted for much. Without any fanfare, my viewpoint shifted. I knew that the policy of barring blacks from the Priesthood was not part of my personal religion. No vascillation this time. No justification. It wasn't right for me, but what could I do? Leave the Church in protest? I didn't want that. But who would listen to me, a non-Priesthood holder, an individual, a woman, a non-Utahn, no less? I would be dismissed as a rebel, agitator or at the very least, an irritant. I didn't want that either. I prayed. I fasted. I cried some more.

One morning, my husband's car would not start. I bundled up two babies, warmed up my car and delivered my husband to work. His office was near the freeway, but I didn't take my usual return route toward home. The steering wheel seemed to guide the way, meandering toward the East Bench hills and turning corners almost of its own volition. When I saw the stalled car in the middle of an East Bench drive, I was surprised. Few ever broke down in suburbia. Then I saw the owner of the crippled car. Black.

What was he doing on the East Bench anyway?

My heart leaped. Maybe I could help. Yes, I could. I didn't need to change any policies or procedures to assist just one person. One person for another. We were there to help each other.

I took him and his tire to a service station, waited for repair and returned him to his car. He thanked me profusely, his eyes smiling. At that moment, I knew that he knew. He had been there just for me.

June 9, 1978. A friend called with the news! "The blacks have just been given the Priesthood."

I called long distance to tell my traveling husband. I called a friend in Connecticut. I called my parents in Nevada.

"Mother, the blacks can hold the Priesthood now."

"Oh. Well, that's nice."

"Isn't it fantastic? I can't believe it's for real."

"Did you hear this from a reliable source?"

I danced. I sang. I cried. My elation even carried me through Sunday School class two days later when the teacher short-circuited every attempt to discuss the revelation, insisting that we stay on the assigned topic.

The prophet had spoken. The silence had been broken.

The "Mormon Cross" had been lifted, and for once, I wasn't out of sync.

Hallelujah. Hallelujah. Al-le-lu-ia!

January 1981. On reflection, was it more important to me that my black brothers and sisters could officially be accepted as equals in the Church organization or was it that I would no longer have to harbor the burning shame or bear the private burden of the perceived prejudice of my church?

In a psychological sense, my encounter with the crippled car on the East Bench had been my absolution, my redemption from *Red Mill* rebuffs, eeney meeney miney moes, and other wrongs committed. My burden had been lifted. The First Presidency had provided the catharsis with the June 9 announcement, and I could sing, "All is well, all is well."

But are things well? As I analyze my own daily behavior, the somber facts are these: I rarely look for people in trouble anymore, black, yellow, white or blue for that matter; I care more about my own family and my own aspirations; I closet myself with pen and paper, with my thoughts about humanity and how *they* could serve each other better.

I have essentially retreated from the cutting edge once again, this time for a different reason: I have been redeemed by one good deed and one official pronouncement.

Oh human nature . . . why does it so often end belly-up, kicking its centipedal legs?

"My job is not my career;
it doesn't occupy
the center of my life.
I have come to view
the whole of my life,
with its multiple components,
as my career."
Jean Wadsworth Johnson

Jerrie W. Hurd

The New Reliable Me

I used to think being a Mormon woman meant baking my own bread, sewing my own quilts and greeting my kids after school every day with nutritious snacks. I hung snowflakes in the gym for Relief Society socials. I substituted in Primary. I drove teenagers to camps and dances. And still I never considered myself good enough. A Mormon woman ought to be more loving to her husband, more understanding with her children, more neighborly to her neighbors, more kind to her dog . . .

I kept trying. When the ward activity committee wanted a poster, I made a poster. When the stake physical fitness specialist needed someone to teach aerobic dancing, I taught aerobic dancing. Imperfect as I was, people counted on me. And I enjoyed the nice little reputation I had for being a reliable person—that is, until it backfired one morning.

It was a Monday. My husband was in the shower. The kids were upstairs getting dressed. I was pouring cornflakes and half listening to the TV news when suddenly I looked up and saw my cousin Lana being interviewed.

I sat down and stared at the TV. I kept thinking, "I'm the same age. I came from the same little town. Lana and I wore lipstick and our first pair of nylons to the same eighth grade dance.

That morning on the TV she wore a trim beige suit. As the designated spokesperson for the National Trucker's Association, a position no woman had ever held before, she was being asked how a nationwide truckers strike might be averted.

Her answer was precise, tough-minded and interesting enough to be aired on the CBS Morning News.

"What's the matter, Mom?" asked one of the kids.

"Nothing."

"You look funny."

"That's because I'm sitting down," I said.

"Oh," he shrugged and tiptoed from the room.

What happened, I wondered, to the girl who had wanted to read *Remembrance of Things Past* all the way to the end? To play Bach on the piano? To become a journalist and travel around the world snapping photos of famous people? And more, much, much more?

"What's the matter?" my husband asked coming in from the kitchen.

I said, "I don't like the way I've turned out."

He yawned. "Oh, you're not so bad."

"I'm serious," I said. "I want to know why we think doing things for others makes us reliable but doing things for ourselves makes us selfish?"

The rest of the morning I moped around in a wallow of self pity. I couldn't see any way out of my dilemma. As a committed Mormon woman, I believed in the sacredness of my marriage and my family. I had no desire to abandon the life I'd made for myself. What I wanted was for someone to take me seriously, to recognize my abilities, to ask me for my opinions. At the same time, I was mature enough to know no one was going to do that.

''Chin up,'' I told myself. ''You know that when ye are in the service of your fellow beings ye are only in the service of your God. Besides in the last days when He comes again in His glory, it's the meek who shall inherit the earth. So endure,'' I told myself, ''endure to the end.''

Yet, even as I gave myself that pep talk, I sensed the bitter undertone and stopped. How did I hope to attain perfection, to become more like Christ, to be fit for His coming kingdom if my endurance and self sacrifice served only to embitter me?

I decided to sit down and list all the things I would do if there were no restrictions on my life. At first I included remodeling the bathroom and paying off the bills. Eventually I crossed those off. I wanted to be honest with myself. If I could do anything, I'd write a novel. I'd teach at the university. I'd travel.

As I worked on my list, I made a deliberate effort to get in touch with myself again. I asked tough questions. What did I enjoy doing? What kind of person did I think I was? Did I ever feel manipulated? By whom? Why? How did I think other people viewed me? Was that how I wanted to be seen? From what source did I draw my sense of self worth and what was I doing to tend and replenish that source?

Gradually as I became better acquainted with myself, I evaluated and adjusted my list until it consisted of twenty-one items. Some were practical, such as wishing I had my own scriptures. Some were more fanciful, such as wanting to hike through Nepal.

Beside each item, I noted what I needed to do to achieve that objective. For example, if I wanted my own scriptures, I had to allow myself the luxury of buying a set instead of feeling that someone (me) ought to squeeze the remaining use out of books my husband had cast aside.

Larger goals required a series of steps. Little by little I was able to construct a definite plan to achieve most of my dearest dreams. That surprised me. Believing that the pursuit of my dreams would be inconsistent with my image of a nurturing Mormon woman, I had avoided identifying the things I really wanted. This blindness had led me to accept limits that did not, in fact, exist.

Now everything seemed clear. The answer was to be more loving to my husband, more understanding to my children, more neighborly to the neighbors, more kind to the dog, more directed in my own goals. Immediately I recognized the old familiar pitfall. In all honesty, I asked myself, how much more could I do than I was already doing?

I looked at my list again. This time I organized my goals along a continuum. Some steps had to come first. I planned to work on some goals while my children were young. I postponed others. In this way, I narrowed my immediate objectives down to two.

Two seemed manageable. Nevertheless, in order to find more time for my new pursuits, I re-examined my church and family commitments. I decided that I would take my turn baking cupcakes for the scouts and driving to seminary but not by sacrificing my own personal goals. I decided to bake bread and do patchwork quilting, but only when I wanted an enjoyable diversion.

Nevertheless, I was naive about the difficulties I faced in returning to my goals. Before marriage I had worked on the staff of a newspaper and I had produced college TV programs. During the intervening years and several moves, I had lost my professional contacts. Even the fact that I had freelanced articles and successfully ventured into certain fiction markets had not helped. I would have to approach the system cold. I would have to prove myself all over again.

Once more, society discounts the time a woman spends with her young children. Once when I put "Chairman of the PTO Spaghetti Dinner" on a resume I drew laughter from members of the Lake Oswego City Council who were considering me for a library board position. Yet as the PTO Dinner Chairman, I had managed a staff of thirteen people and a budget of several thousand dollars, a truly challenging job.

Every woman, whether she is an active feminist or not, must learn to deal with the bias against her. She must recognize both subtle and blatant forms of discrimination, and she must force the issue when it stands in her way. Fortunately many universities and community colleges offer courses for women seeking to re-enter the job market. Part of the training includes learning to phrase one's qualifications in professional terms. That helps, but ironically, my greatest hindrance turned out to be inertia created by my success as a wife, mother and homemaker. My home offered a too-comfortable retreat when facing my professional handicaps got rough. As my early efforts won only repeated rejections, I was forced to search deeper within myself for enough motivation to keep trying. It was then that I discovered I had—as the psychologists say—internalized a double-bind.

I realized that I had half believed my success could only be bought by failure in the home, and since I was unwilling to fail at home, I hadn't expected to succeed. And at the same time, I felt cheated, trapped and unfulfilled by my nurturing role because I knew I was capable of more. I also felt the weight of eternity, with all those spirits waiting to be born into a nice LDS family.

Not all of those feelings came from my church education. I loved reading Jane Austen, George Eliot, Willa Cather and other great women writers. But because I'd identified with them, I'd also identified with their message: bright, exceptional women will suffer social ostracization and rejection. In other words, I half wanted to continue being the down-trodden, the unappreciated, martyr because I'd associated those feelings with putting the family first. I was able to give up that attitude only when I stopped being naive about both the external and the internal difficulties and finally began looking for workable solutions.

In the spring of 1980, I decided to return to the university and pursue an MFA in fiction writing. This was not the safest, easiest choice open to me. It meant making a sizeable investment in tuition and related educational expenses. It meant commuting over one hundred miles once a week. And when I finished, I would have no assurance of a teaching position or of a living made from my writing. Nevertheless, I went back to school, where deciding whether I should be baking cupcakes, studying for finals, rocking a fussing child or fixing supper for the rest of the family became my daily dilemma. Soon after entering the university, I encountered several women who had solved that difficulty by abandoning their family responsibilities. I was glad then for the benefit of priesthood and Relief Society leadership. I could no more have severed my family ties than I could have severed a healthy limb.

Yet I see that my attitude must have appeared unsophisticated. One day as I was trying to juggle my schedule in order to attend my son's piano recital, one of my colleagues asked, "Why do you have to go? Who says your kid's recital is more important than your class?"

"I don't have to go," I said. "I want to go. I enjoy seeing my children perform."

"But you're going to have to choose sometime," she said. "All the good opportunities in this field are in New York and California. When I graduate I plan to go where I can make the best use of my talents. What do you plan to do with your degree?"

At the time I didn't have a good answer. I didn't know how to express my belief in the value of living by eternal principles. I didn't know how to explain the benefit of the balance I was trying to achieve. But later, as I continued to teach at the university, and to write, the advantages of being a committed Mormon woman became more and more evident. While I juggled my schedule around my children's Christmas programs, family home evenings and my husband's travel, my more liberated colleague juggled her schedule around part-time jobs, apartment moves and her roommate's whims. The only real difference was that my activities were more innately satisfying because I was nurturing deep, lasting relationships.

My skills at public speaking, teaching, organizing projects and leading discussion groups also became obvious. I owed that to my years of running a household and working in the church's auxiliaries. The most important advantage, however, was the emotional security I received from my family. That stability allowed me to write with the concentration that enhanced the quality of my work. As the professional status of my work came to be recognized, my colleagues ceased to challenge me and began asking my advice instead.

When the discussion turned from work-related matters to the more nitty-gritty aspects of maintaining an equilibrium in our complex society, I was happy to share my external perspective. Many time I've stood in the middle of my kitchen and asked, "Is it going to matter in the eternal scheme of things if this floor waits another day before being mopped?'' Many times I've sat at my desk and asked myself, ''Is this the most effective thing I can be doing right now?'' As a creature of habit, I've found that unless I keep one eye focused on the longer, larger view, I tend to slip into meaningless routines. Yet even with the best planning, I've often had to choose between two equally good activities simply because there wasn't time to do both. In those cases, I have asked myself, ''Which would I most enjoy doing?''

My colleagues found this application of my religious beliefs to the mundane aspects of my life intriguing. I think I have opened more missionary doors by discussing the merits of finding time to teach my son's cub scout troop than I ever did in long philosophical discussions.

It has been three years since the morning my cousin's appearance on TV jolted me out of my complacency. In that time, I have accomplished two of my objectives and made progress toward achieving two others more than I had thought possible in such a short time.

I am glad I confronted my personal ambitions. Without that confrontation, I might have settled for less than I could have achieved. Not that I'm euphoric. I have no grand illusions. Even with my goals firmly in mind and a plan to achieve them, I still have bad days and miserable disappointments. Although I still have fond dreams I'll never achieve, I do believe I will come closer than I would have if I had never been so candid with myself.

As I began working on my goals, I felt happier, happier because I was doing what I really enjoyed. The day I sold my first short story, I was so engrossed in working on a new story that I didn't even open the acceptance letter until evening. The process of working on my goals has become as satisfying as their accomplishment.

My family was the first to notice my improved attitude. Yet if I was to continue, I knew I needed more than their appreciation—I needed their support. In a frank family home evening discussion, I pointed out the stake they had in my cheerier disposition. No woman can be a successful, loving, cheerful wife, mother and professional and still do all the laundry, all the cooking, all the dishes and all the errands. I told my family that if they wanted me to continue being a reasonably cheerful person, they would have to help.

They responded by reminding me that in the past when they had tried to help, I had insisted that they do things my way and according to my standards. They made it clear that they considered that demeaning. I had to admit that my attitude had been self-defeating, so this time we divided the chores into autonomous units. My husband took complete responsibility for the bathrooms and the yard. One son took complete responsibility for the vacuuming and the dusting. We agreed that each individual could execute his or her responsibilities however and whenever each wished as long as the chores were done often enough and well enough to satisfy the majority of the other family members.

I wish I could say that having specific assignments made our transition easy. As the novelty wore off, however, those who had grown used to expecting Mom to accommodate their comforts found it easy to slip back into old habits. Even I found myself indulging in old attitudes. But with patience, a continuing commitment and a willingness to work together toward better solutions, our whole family has come a long way toward sharing responsibilities equally.

One night as my husband and I sat alone on the couch

watching an old romantic movie on the TV, I cozied up to him and said, ''I've finally figured it out.''

''What's that?'' he asked.

''The answer to my question.''

''What question?''

''Why do we think doing things for others makes us reliable but doing things for ourselves makes us selfish?''

''And what's the answer?''

''It isn't selfish. Think about it. Anyone who develops his or her talents will not only have a better self but better skills to share. Besides, if every woman baked bread and made quilts, who'd teach, who'd discover new cures, who'd officiate at school board meetings and who'd act the comic blond roles for movies like this one?''

He laughed. ''See, I told you. You're not so bad.''

RevaBeth Russell

A Purple Rose

A vivid memory of my youth is as a Mia-Maid at Rose Night: How tense I became when the sweet girls chose white or pink or red roses, with the appropriate moral values from the lesson manual how irritated when they couldn't find a purple rose for me to add to the bouquet. I remember saying, "I choose this yellow rose because they couldn't find a purple rose. I choose a purple rose because it is unique, yet beautiful. It is unparallelled in its effort to excel in a field where it is so alone. I will be myself and think for myself."

In a field of lily white roses I've always felt like a purple one. I can visualize myself in the pre-existence complaining about the necessity of an appendix in a mortal body, or insisting that my heavenly name be spelled differently from the millions of others. To my non-Mormon friends I appear normal-Mormon. I teach a class of 13 and 14 year-olds in Sunday School, attend Relief Society, direct ward plays, bake my own bread and love quilting. I sew the family's clothing, grow and bottle my own vegetables in the fall. I am very defensive about anything infringing on my night with my family and have even admitted that I would like another child.

To my normal-Mormon friends I appear almost apostate. I am president of the community women's organization that raised money for respectable causes such as the mentally retarded and the local hospital but has also raised money for "evil" projects such as sex education in the schools and birth control information. Last year I was chairwoman of the club's Las Vegas gambling night where we earned eleven thousand dollars at poker, craps, blackjack and roulette. I have said no to many ward requests—other than those to which I have committed myself through a specific calling. I have been chastised for missing an impromptu pre-planning Relief Society meeting when it conflicted with my long-standing commitment to play piano at a nursing home. (I wasn't "furthering the work of the Lord.") I have even refused to host Tupperware parties.

I have goals for myself as a person, wife, mother, community leader and church member, and so to keep my sanity, I have decided to choose exactly which directives I will obey. I choose to attend a city council meeting rather than work on my genealogy. I choose between limiting my family to three right now instead of becoming the raving maniac mother of four. I choose exactly how many items I can comfortably make for the ward bazaar to show my support while still allowing myself time to get my Christmas ready in a cheerful manner. I even posted some scriptures, I can honestly say I read them every day.

When I read stories out of the manuals, whether Primary, Relief Society, or Family Home Evening, the decisions always seem to be black and white. Everything fits into place for the white rose in the lesson. Maybe because I am a purple rose all of the issues in my life are gray.

The Santa Fe community was recently involved in a

heated controversy over sex education in the schools. I had previously taught sex education on a volunteer basis. I agreed with the sex education group who pointed out the documented ignorance of the youth in this area and how ignorance had and would lead to unwanted pregnancies. But this same pro-sex education group shows films advising young people not to go to their parents for help. The anti-sex education group warns that sex education would only whet the appetites of the youth to learn more. I disagree with that argument but can see their reason for protesting the distribution of pamphlets advocating masturbation. During this controvesy, several ladies in the ward wanted me to help drive sex education from the classroom. The pro-sex education group wanted me to help keep the curriculum in the classroom. I felt in the middle, not being able to champion either side but able to see points of view, and pleading for a middle ground. Be it ERA, Common Cause or Birthright, I am never at peace.

I don't fit the mold at home either. I hear that President McKay and his wife never had a cross word. In a Sacrament Meeting a Seventies' president declares that his marriage is perfect—and I know mine isn't, and it would be wrong to pretend that my husband and I don't ever fight. I struggle with the fact that I can't be a perfect member of the Church and that all of my petals aren't perfect. I will often reach the boiling point and yell at my kids—after a Relief Society lesson on how to maintain a perfectly reverent mood in the home. (I even yell when non-member neighbors are out in their yards). Maybe it's because I know I'm not perfect that I resent being called "Sister Russell." (The real reason, I suspect though, is that the identity represented by my first name and maiden name is lost).

Life challenges me to juggle my selfish goals. I insist on doing my best when I teach or conduct a meeting, and this means many hours of preparation. I also insist on the same quality time for my children. I love their active bodies. I love kissing the sleep from them. I love their refreshing outlook on the world: ("Everybody lived with Jesus before they were born, even murderers and robbers"). I love teaching them the love of Christ and listening to their simple prayers ("And bless Grandma Loveridge that when she is resurrected she won't have cancer again"). Amid the work, laundry, the constant prattle, special diets, and emergency room visits in the middle of the night, there is no greater thrill than a loud, off-key, but sincere rendition of "Mother, I lo-o-v-e you-u. Mother I do-o-o."

But my entire seventy years or so on earth won't be spent chasing a little nude body down the hall to diaper it, or proudly taking pictures of the cutest kid at the school program or worrying about the teen out with the car. For me there are so many things to learn, to see, to experience and to master that I refuse to cloister myself in one role. Somewhere I picked up the notion that I can do anything, and I thank my parents, teachers and husband for that priceless gift—it keeps the limits ever-changing and challenging.

I view myself as struggling, trying not to fall in a rut or mold. I would cringe if someone told me I look Mormon. I must admit that I don't feel as I expect a Mormon woman to feel, yet being Mormon is as much me as being a woman. Now and then I have resented being Mormon as much as I resent my monthly menstrual cycle, but I would not undergo a Mormonectomy any more than I would an unnecessary hysterectomy. Both together help make me.

Jean Wadsworth Johnson

Life Beyond the Pumpkin Shell

Peter, Peter, Pumpkin Eater,
Had a wife and couldn't keep her.
Put her in a pumpkin shell
And there he kept her very well.

In spite of periodic cycles of stress and conflict, I had been very well kept for most of the twenty-five years of my marriage in a comfortably furnished pumpkin shell with a view. Whenever my capabilities caught up with the challenges, I would begin to feel the vague restlessness of wondering what more I could do with my life. Each time I chose to have another child instead of expanding my activities beyond my home, church and neighborhood school. When divorce dispossessed me and the remaining four of six children from our pumpkin shell style of life, I faced the prospect, at age 46, of evolving from a bread baker to a bread winner with no previous work experience outside my home. I have a B.S. degree in nursing, but I had never practiced, having made a joint commitment with my husband at the time of our marriage that our children would have a full-time, at-home mother. But new beginnings, even if involuntary, offer opportunities for new choices. I had loved my training as a student nurse, but that choice had been made when I was eighteen years old. I asked myself the question, "What work would I choose if I could do whatever I wanted to do?" That seemed a simple question, but it took weeks of prayerful thought for the answer to formulate in my mind. I began thinking that I wanted to work at something to which I could apply my years of experience as a parent, homemaker and active member of the church. The answer came: I wanted to work with youth.

In my community, if you want to work with youth, you logically apply at the local state correctional facility for adolescent offenders. Corrections itself held little appeal for me, but I reasoned that kids are kids, and you take them where you find them. When, for the first time in my life, I filled out a job application, I rebelled at leaving blank the spaces provided for previous experience. I filled them in with description of what I had done as a parent, homemaker, church worker, and community volunteer. Where it asked for the beginning salary of my last job, I wrote "Love." My shaking hand was not nearly as assertive as my words, but I hoped that the productiveness of those twenty-five years would speak for me.

Evidently, the information on my application did make a favorable impression, not because of the experience it described, but probably because it showed that I place a high value upon those skills and believe I have something useful to offer in the position. I was interviewed and hired as a night counselor in the girl's cottage and therefore entered a course of education directed toward a degree in full adulthood. In our society, and particularly within the

Mormon culture, there are seeming rewards of love and protection for the woman who remains, in some respects, a child-like, semi-adult. Unconsciously I had made such a bargain. Being employed exposed me to the realities of time structure, money management, accountability to supervision, working relationships and new ideas. In working with delinquent adolescent girls, I had to recognize realities in our society that had seemed remote and abstract when viewed from the shelter of my pumpkin shell. I came to realize that most of these girls were victims before they became offenders. Their life stories revealed varying degrees of neglect, rejection, and abuse that included rape and incest. They were left with such a poor self-image that they often believed they had deserved the treatment and so they actually perpetuated the treatment by becoming involved in juvenile prostitution and other offenses.

To train for my job, I attended workshops of rape, incest, juvenile prostitution and battered women which not only changed my perspective on my own experience but gave me a broader understanding of the girls I served. What I learned caused me to face the reality of the circumstances in which I too had been a battered wife. I had always minimized the impact of these episodes on my self esteem and on my marriage, but through these workshops, I came to a better understanding of the dynamics of battering, and I stopped accepting the blame. I also became more aware of the subtle attitudes in our society that create a climate where victimization of women and children can occur. I am now convinced that the Church needs to recognize the serious consequences of sexist attitudes. The Gospel of Jesus Christ assumes the equality of men and women. Jesus did not teach it to women through male interpreters. He did not patronize nor talk down to women of the Bible. Generations of programming have contaminated the relationships of equality, and sexist values cannot be automatically washed away in the waters of baptism.

I was increasingly uneasy with the attitudes of some of the male staff who seemed to be either discounting or patronizing in their interaction with the girl students. Those attitudes seemed counterproductive in equipping the girls to take responsibility for their lives. I knew them to be daughters of a loving Father in Heaven, and I desired to serve them by treating them fairly and by teaching them and encouraging them to conduct their lives more effectively. It was no simple task to move toward these objectives while coping with the often destructive patterns of behavior they showed as a result of their rebelliousness, hostility, anxiety, and lack of trust and self-esteem.

Running away from painful situations and responsibility had become an established pattern with many of the students, so security and the prevention of escapes from our open cottage and campus was always a problem. We cannot treat them if we cannot keep them there, and the situation of runaways on the streets leaves them vulnerable to exploitation. One night, Susan streaked past the pool of light from my desk lamp and ran down the darkened stairs. Just behind her ran Linda, a girl newly admitted for assault. I had suspected that Susan might try to persuade the new girl to run with her, and I was determined to prevent it. I grabbed Linda's arm and hung on as we bounced down the stairs together. She seemed surprised that I would not let go of her arm as she struggled to free herself from this crazy lady. As she raised her unencumbered arm, I read in her face the fleeting temptation to strike me. But she chose not to. She soon stopped struggling and returned to her room. When Susan realized that Linda had failed to follow her, she too returned to the dorm.

I soon found myself in similar situations completely foreign to my previous experience. I had to put out a fire a girl had started in the mattress of her lock-up room. I received a bloody nose from trying to restrain one girl from hitting another. I talked a girl out of the woods one rainy night after she had cut her wrists and run away. Although there were times when I suffered from emotional "pumpkin shell bends," I found I could handle these situations without shattering. The professionalism I learned in my nurses training proved to be an important asset in coping with difficult circumstances and disturbed personalities.

Support from my co-workers was slow in coming. My young women colleagues were not enthusiastic about working with a woman as old as their mothers, but in time, we became friends. Some men at the institution still consider women an intrusion, but two of the night counselors and the night supervisor were helpful. It was a year, however, before I received any positive feedback about my work. I had always depended upon reassurance from others for my confidence and self-worth. The absence of this vital ingredient led to a crucial adjustment in my modus operandi. I found that I had to make up my own mind about the effectiveness of my work, do what I thought best in carrying out the treatment objectives of the staff team, and stand by it.

After I had changed from night shift to day shift, I received a negative evaluation. My supervisor had documented every time I disagreed with a policy or an assessment of a situation in the planning meetings. Not only did he use my verbal disagreement to give me a low rating, but he said my facial expressions betrayed my lack of compliance. I therefore learned to be more guarded and diplomatic although I felt frustrated at not being allowed any real input in decisions about the girls. When the girl's program was terminated, I was disappointed and discouraged. I had thought my calling was working with girls.

A few months later, a new program was announced at my institution for re-entry rehabilitation of minimum security adult males from two state prisons. I applied and was surprised to be accepted. It was stimulating to work together in developing the program from its inception and in modifying it as we worked with the residents. My supervisors were impressed by my ability to relate to these men and establish my authority in supervising them. As the only woman counselor on the staff for this unit, my age was an asset in this situation. No one on the staff knew what to expect of adult felons. In the process of adapting the program, I discovered some organizational skills as well. My supervisors considered my suggestions and insights, causing me to feel more equality as a team member. We were amazed to find that these young adults were not greatly different from the juvenile boys. We had been led to expect greater sophistication and resistance to treatment components. Although I had parted reluctantly with girls, I found that working with boys was not as dissimilar as I had anticipated. I have come to believe that we all experience common needs for recognition, acceptance, self-expression and safety regardless of age or sex. It is when children or adults become discouraged in meeting these needs that they resort to negative, destructive behavior.

Although this program was successful, it too was terminated by a new commissioner who did not want adults and juveniles on the same campus. We resumed our work with boys.

A good evaluation of my work with adults put me on the list for promotion. The director of the adult program who was made program director for the facility offered me the opportunity to become a group leader. I refused the position because the working hours would have kept me away from home during the supper and early evening hours. Later I accepted the position as cottage manager. There had never been a woman in a supervisory position within the treatment program at this institution so it created some controversy. The feminist movement made it possible for the entry of women into positions as staff serving male clients, and publicized the dearth of women in supervisory positions in state employ. Affirmative action quotas may not be an ideal solution, but without them, the door would remain closed.

As a cottage manager, I fill in for absent cottage team members and sometimes for the manager. I work shifts as a counselor and lead groups in meetings or fill in for the director of our unit. I enjoy the variety of tasks and the flexible hours, but I sometimes feel ignored or discounted by my colleagues who make me aware that I am a grandmother working in a young man's world. My supervisor, a kindly man and a dedicated professional, sometimes fails to introduce me when making a round of introductions to visitors. This slight is not deliberate but I have come to view it as symbolic of his need to regard my services as inconsequential. Because I am often bypassed in the flow of information I sometimes make mistakes that cause me to appear inept. I have been frustrated because my supervisory responsibilities were not clearly defined, but this is in the process of being clarified in my job description. To shrug off my anger about these situations simply perpetuates them.

It has been my observation that should a man stumble and fall, he will likely curse the uneven sidewalk and complain to city officials. Should a woman stumble and fall on the same uneven sidewalk, she is more likely to self-consciously laugh at her own clumsiness.

I have been conditioned to believe that an angry woman is unlovely, unlovable and certainly un-Mormon, but I have had to recognize that I do feel anger which, in reality, is more aptly described as deep rage. Some of this rage is left over from the way I was programmed to dependency and compliancy in my parental home although I dearly love my parents. Some of this rage was generated by the tyranny of my husband which resulted in divorce. Some I trace to the times the counsel of the priesthood was insensitive and misdirected. The top layer of rage is the result of occasions when I am not taken seriously by my co-workers. I have learned that I can recognize this rage and give it a name without acting upon it nor allowing it to nourish an attitude of bitterness, the most futile of all emotions. Instead, I have used it to observe myself, to try to understand what I am doing to invite discounting. I found myself often in a posture of self-effacement, waiting for permission to do my job—waiting to be included. In my concern to be non-threatening and compliant, I had been waiting to be assigned a working role on the team, overlooking opportunities to become responsible for my own productivity within the structure. I can discipline my rage to power the assertiveness necessary to be more effective.

Within my pumpkin shell, I directed my unconscious rage at myself, becoming suicidally depressed. When I emerged from my pumpkin shell, I was tempted to direct my rage at others, also destructive and ineffective, blighting any possibility for happiness or peace of mind. I now try to transform this rage into the courage and energy needed for change that I might overcome constricting habits of thought and behavior to more fully realize my potential as a unique child of God.

It has helped me to recognize the correlation of working situations to team sports. Some of the rules are written, but most are unwritten and unspoken. It takes awareness to discern the rules, but when you start playing by them, they will work for you. When you are "fouled," you can call it and it will usually be acknowledged. If you don't use the rules, you are in the "game" but only as a pawn. As women working in a man's world, we are handicapped by our limited experience with team sports. We tend to take the "plays" personally, reacting to them rather than objectively countering them to achieve the goal. Some employees play a defensive game to protect their "backfield," to prevent others from scoring, and to prevent others from raising expectations.

I attempt to play a conservatively offensive game with my goal being to influence the policies and environment of our cottage to provide our clients the greatest possibility for change in their behavior patterns. The most important quality I bring to the task is an enthusiastic willingness to serve. Enthusiasm has led me to volunteer for committees such as the core team for assessing the need to address the chemical use problems in the treatment plans of the students. Cottage managers consequently, were trained to do chemical use problem assessments, and thus an effective area of expertise was added to my job description.

It is interesting that the archaic meaning of enthusiasm

is "inspired by God." I believe that enthusiasm is one quality of the power in Moroni 7:3 "And Christ hath said: If ye will have faith in me ye shall have power to do whatsoever thing is expedient in me." Enthusiasm requires a high level of energy be maintained only by observing personal disciplines. For me, these have proved to be a sugar-free diet, daily jogging, scripture reading and prayer. One comfort of a pumpkin shell life was that if I was irresponsible in one area, there was someone to take up the slack. There was always someone I could blame when excusing myself from having family prayer or reading the scriptures. I could say to myself, "I would be more spiritual if my husband were more diligent." I could use the same excuse for not exercising or going on a diet. I now have to accept full responsibility for my own physical, mental and spiritual health.

Working in the world as a single woman has increased my awareness for the need to build and maintain a network of relationships for mutual emotional support. This can be difficult in any organization where high anxiety levels breed mistrust. Even superficial congeniality, however, can be an effective part of an emotional network and is worth cultivating. I have a few trusted friends who supply reciprocal acceptance, understanding and humor. "And that same sociality which exists among us here will exist among us there, only it will be coupled with eternal glory, which glory we do not now enjoy." There are times when all sources of support can seem to let you down no matter how carefully you have tried to maintain them. Recently I made the rounds of my network and collected stings instead of strokes, but the expected depression did not come. Instead came the realization that while it was not pleasant, I could forebear and choose not to succumb to my neediness. I rejoiced at this significant step toward true adulthood.

It may seem that I exchanged my pumpkin shell for a career, but I do not perceive it in that light. Undue emphasis is given what we do for a living by naming it a career. Such emphasis makes us vulnerable to a needlessly painful loss of identity if we are fired or retired. My job is not my career: it does not occupy the center of my life. I have come to view the whole of my life, with its multiple components, as my career. While some aspects of it were unwholesome, to regret my years in my pumpkin shell seems disloyal to me and my children. I am no superwoman and I doubt that I could have raised six children without the security of a pumpkin shell while they were young. My pumpkin shell memories and lessons are a portion of my lifetime career and cannot be discounted. "To everything there is a season, and a time to every purpose under heaven." These are the lessons of this season of my life; no more nor less important than the lessons of past seasons nor of seasons yet to come.

Marilyn Curtis White

Directions: Cart Trails to Freeways

A 1000-pound black and white "Elsie," pastured behind our house came over the sagging back fence and made for the highway, causing immediate panic among early Sunday motorists. Shooing the animal back into my yard, I placed a squadron of children at the open ends that permit access to the road and phoned the owners. They would be "right down" they said, but when it came time for us to leave for church, they had not yet arrived.

Taking a rope, I fashioned it into the only knot I knew how to make, a slip knot, and in fright approached the beast and flung the loop over her head. I fastened the other end to a post and left for Church, thinking the owners would be there momentarily and in the meantime, motorists would be safe. Upon my return I found the owners standing soberly over their dead animal. How was I, a girl born and raised in Washington D.C., supposed to know a cow might pull the rope tight and choke to death rather than take a step forward and let the rope slacken.

The Lord showed great wisdom when he saw fit not to make me a pioneer mother. It seems to me that we are all born to different tracks and whether or not they head over mountains depends on the map each of us is given to follow. I have walked the old trails of pioneer art to find my beginnings and bearings. I once knit a coat, and because handmade wool things never wear out, grew to hate it. I thought of my pioneer great grandmother possibly looking at an oft-worn dress with undoubtedly the same ill will I was feeling. I finally appeased my conscience by giving it to Deseret Industries. I make bread with a bread mixer and cook a lot from scratch (no packaged mix feeds nine), and I sew for my seven children (who could afford not to?), but last year I gave up sewing for myself. I decided I would rather have one superb outfit than a closet full of makeshift dresses.

Here in Hawaii a pineapple field was being closed out to make room for a freeway extension. I joined with the neighborhood in fighting the sharp spikes of the plants for the ripened fruit. We then had to skin and cut it to be bottled, frozen, made into fruit leather, dried or jammed. The acid from the fruit burned great sores on our hands as I thought about Great Grandmother's hands marked and red from her years of labor. Where pioneer women excelled in such tasks as these, I do not. When I do them, it is only out of necessity, never love.

I heard a speaker say the other day that with our modern technology we have half the work our forebears had, but we take twice as long to accomplish it. I often see this in Mormon homes. Women spread housekeeping chores over the entire day, even refusing other activities because of these tasks. To me a clean house and completed household duties are only a means to an end: freeing my time to develop other talents with which the Lord has blessed me. I have thought too, that perhaps, this is why there is frustration among LDS women. They have limited themselves to the tasks of a former generation when their maps clearly lead them in other directions.

I have one talent no ancestor of mine ever shared. At Brigham Young University, I wrote sports articles for the newspaper. It was not a "fashionable" thing to do in the early sixties, and I was blatantly discriminated against. I was refused a seat in all NCAA press boxes. Even though I was Associate Sports Editor, I was continually passed over, with promotions going to less-qualified male reporters.

The pioneers had dealt with discrimination in their own way, but since there are no more Zions to flee to, I had to take my stand in the world as it was. At first discrimination did not keep me from doing what I loved—writing about the competitive world. But without promotion my assignments were of less and less significance. Only when I could no longer develop my talent did I decide to challenge the system. When I met with the faculty advisor and administrative representative I was surprised to find that the idea that women sports reporters were discriminated against had never occurred to them. I was assured that the press box ruling served to protect me from the offensive language therein. When I pointed out that no one had ever protected me from the offensive language of the fans and that I needed access to statistical information available only at the press box, they sought to have the NCAA ruling changed. But it was long years in coming. The sole argument against my promotion to Sports Editor was that I could not do in-locker room interviews; otherwise, I was doing the other work of the position and doing it well. I won the position when I pointed out that we hadn't done a single in-locker room interview all year. Then, even though the administration was willing to be reasonable, I discovered more subtle difficulties in being taken seriously.

Once when Gene Fullmer, then the "Middleweight Champion of the World," was working in Provo, I was sent to interview him. He gave an excellent interview to the only girl at ringside. What came out the next day was not my in-depth study of a dynamic man, but a "cutsie" piece about a frail female sportswriter breaking down long-held masculine bastions. It was the beginning of the end. After college I left sports writing for straight reporting because "the cause" was roadblocking my potential.

These experiences made me realize that changes are needed in our world, in and out of the Church, if women are to reach their potential. Yet feminists, out to end discrimination, failed to open new options—limiting them instead. They pitted woman against woman seeming to value career women above homemakers and mothers. "Either or" was not enough for me. I wanted it all. My career went into a holding pattern when I married and began to raise my seven children, but unlike many Mormon women who dropped into their homes and were never heard from again, I kept up my writing. I now edit a monthly newsletter for a state organization and have published short stories, poems, articles and songs.

Being a housewife and mother has been not confining but liberating. Had I continued in a career, I would never have had the control over my time that I do now. My paths are not limited to a single direction but are branched. I paint in oils, cook Mexican and Chinese food, do genealogical research, and continue to keep informed on what is happening in the world. When women's rights became the cause of the decade, I was eager to become involved too. There were still inequities to be rectified, and I believed that because the Gospel had given me an understanding of women's role, I could help effect change that would magnify that role rather than curtail it.

In Hawaii our International Women's Year Conference was well attended by Mormon women. Because I knew parliamentary procedure, I was chosen to act as parliamentarian for the "Traditionalists," as we came to be called. Because of the influx of Mormons, a complete slate of "traditional" women was elected to represent the state at the national IWY in Houston. We also prevented Hawaii from going on record in support of abortion, gay rights and the ERA. Any losses we suffered were of our own making. I saw Mormon women chosen as leaders, who over the pulpit and in the name of Jesus Christ told their sisters to watch their lead and vote "no" as a bloc on every issue. I was one of a few who walked out of that meeting where the misuse of sudden power overwhelmed one of the basic tenets of our faith—free agency. I saw sisters so ignorant of the issues that they couldn't do anything but blindly follow their leaders. I saw LDS women so afraid of those who did not hold their point of view that they refused to engage in honest debate. And afterward, I saw Mormon women go back into their houses and shut the doors on a world they had only glimpsed and had refused to confront.

Where our grandmothers had worlds to conquer within their homes, I believe we have worlds to conquer beyond our homes. The Church knows more about the way a woman should chart her life than the world does, and so it seems to me that if we are to have an impact on that world, we must share this knowledge at many levels. I've shed my flowered mumuus for business suits to appear as a lobbyist at the State Legislature. I sometimes leave my children while I educate other women on the issues. I have even had to excuse myself from a Church assignment in order to debate on television and radio. As a Relief Society President with four other Church callings, I have had to learn to say, "no" and then have had to overcome the guilt feelings that follow.

My husband and children are the bane of my existence, but they remain my first priority and always the eternal work of my life. Because I am still maintaining such a large family, I limit myself to active involvement in only one community organization. For the few months out of the year when the Legislature is in session, our home gets hectic. Though some things pile up, I've found that many things will keep for later attention. My children pass petitions, scan newspaper articles, gather information, and take over household chores while I attend hearings. Not long ago my sixteen-year-old daughter stood up and asked a legislative committee to fund other important programs instead of additional sex counseling in her school. My husband and I think it is important to teach our children how to defend the principles they believe in.

I have found that it is no longer enough to bake, sew, and clean. Technology has created room in our lives for more accomplishments than Grandmother was able to do. We must not fail to embark on these other stewardships, made possible through that gift of time. I weep for the Relief Society sister who in a lesson on chastity announced that a "virtuous woman" should keep her eyes cast down lest she look a Priesthood bearer in the eye and cause improper feelings between them; I wince when a husband forbids his wife to attend a BYU-Hawaii campus Women's Conference because she must leave her children with a sitter for two days; I hurt when a Stake Relief Society President bans the showing of informative films on depression and Mormon women because they might cause an increase in birth control practices.

Last summer we took our children to visit the ranch their Great Grandfather homesteaded in McKinnon, Wyoming. They need to appreciate what went before, as I do. But the trails blazed by our grandparents were largely physical; mine are intellectual, my children's yet uncharted, but all are spiritual; and the same strength that led the pioneers across the desert, I believe, will continue to lead me.

Dolores Ritchie

"When April with its Sweet Showers"

"Mademoiselle, hasn't anyone told you it isn't safe for a woman to travel alone in France?" The glinty-eyed, middle-aged, Lothario-styled ticket agent of Limoges was not the first to ask the question. When several years ago I determined that this was the year for "breaking away," only my family accepted this decision to embark on my long dreamed-of pilgrimage to the churches of medieval France. Fearing for my safety, many anxious friends and some relatives offered to accompany me, no doubt seeing in my voyage the portent of calamities read about in Gothic novels and cheap scandal sheets. My daughter, then seventeen, had the best response when answering her skeptical friend's disbelief: "Oh no? You don't know my mother!"

Actually, the idea of the trip had been developing for several years while I had been studying French and medieval art and history. The "frame" of the trip grew out of my love of Chaucer's pilgrims who, with the "sweet showers" of spring, set out on their journey to holy places such as Canterbury. I perhaps shared too much their naive faith and love of adventure, or why else would I plan a two-months' journey to the major Romanesque and Gothic churches of France?

And why did I decide to travel alone with all the risks that such a trip would engender, you ask? On one level it grew out of a purely aesthetic and academic yearning to experience a kind of medieval pilgrimage, a journey to "stranger strands" and "sundry lands." I, of course, would have preferred to join a company of friends or shared the experience with loved ones, but I found no one whose interest, time, or compatibility of purpose matched my own.

On a second level, perhaps simply born out of necessity, I traveled alone to prove something to myself, and as such it became a personal pilgrimage—a "rite of passage," of sorts. Perhaps I am not alone in modeling several quite contradictory images, forged sometimes in fact, sometimes in fiction. Friends see me as confident, my family and children as brazen and unpredictable. *I* know that my confidence is laced with self-doubt, though paradoxically mixed with reckless optimism. The two warring elements came into focus during the course of my travels and were revealed, on one level, in my need for personal acceptance and self-mastery, (a kind of "security" dimension), and in my need for challenge and adventure (a "risk" dimension) on another level.

These seemingly disparate needs were constantly at play in my journey. For instance, I had spent months preparing for the trip, reading travel books and French railway schedules; sifting through books and articles on history, architecture, and sculpture; pursuing French through tapes and texts; and reducing my information into a compact black book neatly organized for the retrieval of almost anything. For months I had been studying the

National Geographic map of medieval France, pinpointing major churches and cities of both Roman Gaul and the France of Eleanor of Aquitaine and her troubadour ancestors. I devised a series of three to seven-day trips from several major centers: London and Paris, where I had friends living; and Nantes, where I would have the house and car of a French family with whom we were exchanging homes for the month of July.

But lest I get carried away with the projection of myself as the complete traveler, I must stop to reveal where my desire for security met head-on with my love of adventure and risk. I arrived in London only to find that my friends were already unexpectedly putting up another traveler. Feeling reluctant to crowd them, I decided to spend a few days traveling north where lay one of my pilgrimage goals, Durham Cathedral.

Since I would be gone only a few days, I decided to travel light, carrying only my black denim satchel (which passed for everywoman's marketing bag), containing a nightgown, a change of clothes and my personal items. But I had also decided to change from a heavy leather purse, to a lighter, woven one, and in so doing I had forgotten the secret pocket of the leather purse which held my traveler's checks. Consequently, I found myself on a bus leaving London for a three-day journey with only eleven dollars. Because returning would have meant a day's delay and an embarrassing explanation, I decided to "wing it." I would rely on my "never leave home without it," American Express card.

At my first stop, the quaint half-timbered town of Chester, I learned that the nearest bank to honor an American Express card was at York, some eighty miles east and accessible only by bus the next day. Realizing that

Chester's most modest "bed and breakfast" accommodations would be beyond my means, I boarded the first bus headed east. It was now early evening as I joined weary commuters who no doubt worked in Chester's booming tourist businesses though they lived in the nearby metropolis of Liverpool. Since the bus was continuing on to Manchester and finally Leeds (only twenty-five miles from York), I decided to stop there overnight. I doubt there are three more depressing cities in England at twilight, or so I imagined it as we traveled the typically degenerating back streets of those industrial cities, made more miserable by my fatigue, hunger, and apprehension.

People began to thin out as the darkness grew. Soon there were only the bus driver and his assistant, a loquacious woman who obviously knew the driver well enough to discuss vacation plans, health problems and mutual friends in an almost incomprehensible English dialect. They became inquisitive about my destination, and after some friendly banter I asked them if they could recommend a "bed and breakfast" in Leeds. Since we would not arrive there until after 9:00 p.m., the driver offered to direct me to an area near the station which had such accommodations. When we reached our destination, he walked me to several of them, but some were full, and others too depressing for consideration.

The driver, no doubt sensing my precarious situation, offered to let me stay in his flat where, because his wife was out of town, there would be plenty of room. Now he who had seemed to be my friend suddenly became frighteningly suspicious. It grew darker and I began to see malevolence at every turn. The next stop was equally foreboding, or so it seemed to me, but the manager of the premises who greeted us belied its appearance. In her eagerness to help she took me by the hand and embraced me with proffers of food and protection. From my trembling she must have suspected that I felt threatened by the bus driver who accompanied me and hurried me in to her protective custody.

Looking back, I believe that the bus driver was sincere in his attempts to help, but at the time I was too desolate to hold back the tears that were an almost certain indictment against him. I perhaps naively believed that the problem was not "out there" so much as it was in me—my anger at being trapped by mismanagement and the shame I felt at not keeping my "risks" within safe limits.

Perhaps this risk-taking is not unfamiliar to others who have been raised to "play games" in various aspects of their lives, and sometimes at high cost. Just as the risks I took sometimes revealed an almost cavalier disregard for personal safety, so do those who would climb precarious peaks, hang-glide, or the numerous other "games" that pose for many of us a way to measure ourselves against precarious odds.

One aspect of the "game" for me was working through some of my self-doubt with its accompanying paralysis of action. I met this challenge by realizing that I had the choice to take charge of doing something very important to me—taking a trip to France alone. Always before when traveling I had depended on my husband to read maps and plane schedules. Alone now, facing a brusque ticket agent in a foreign land, shouting insecurely to penetrate the deafening noise, I found that I could meet such a trial successfully. Map-reading—another minor conquest—seems equally trivial unless one realizes that heretofore it had always been a "turn it upside down to see if one goes left or right" proposition. Every new thing—choosing

Hovercraft over the ferry between Dover, England and France—was my decision and my challenge.

The validation of self-worth, in the absence of identifying husband and children, another paradox to my public image of brazen self-confidence, came through various one-to-one experiences with the French people. On my first day's train trip in France, I met a girl my daughter's age. Being a little homesick I emerged from my usual comfortable anonymity and engaged her in conversation. She was intrigued with my pilgrimage, and in our half-English, half-French conversation there emerged our common love of literature and philosophy. When we arrived at her destination, Amiens, she walked me to the cathedral and we shared a warm and most affectionate "Adieu."

It was always a challenge to expose my vulnerability to the proverbially aloof French stranger. However, I often found them warm and responsive to a "damsel in distress," especially when adventure and expediency led me to ask for rides from strangers. Such was the case one day in Laon when it became apparent that my goal of visiting three cathedrals in one day was impossible. Seeing a small family approaching the parking lot of the Laon Cathedral, I swallowed my pride and asked if they were by chance driving to Rheims. At first they looked at me suspiciously, but I hurriedly explained who I was, "a professor from the United States, studying in France for several months." They made room for me, and while traveling I explained my pilgrimage and they grew more friendly and inquisitive. I found it hopeless to tell people that I was from Utah—it is not yet on the international map—so I usually said that I was from San Francisco (my real, if not present, home). Invariably this caught their interest and gave me credibility. Later as we made our separate ways through the cathedral, I passed the family and we shared warm smiles in a friendship forged so quickly in a dialogue that encompassed our mutual love of the treasured cathedrals of France and the great cities of our countries.

Another encounter during the journey had a much more menacing beginning. I had been wandering through the small town of Souillac (with its marvelous abbey sculptures of the 11th century). I had arrived there in the early evening and began a circuit of the town. After visiting the church I stumbled onto an intriguing cemetery near the outskirts of town. It was very unlike anything I had seen before: above-ground tombs crowded together like an abandoned city and each tomb adorned with the most bizarre funerary decorations. Perhaps the late hour gave rise to the sound of chains rattling and shrieking of an owl (maybe it was shades of the Dickens' novel found in an obscure French used-bookstore that called these images to mind). Feeling that I'd better return to my hotel before dark and hoping that the opposite side of the cemetery would yield a faster route back, I made that choice and a long walk, only to find a deadend. And it was almost dark! Hurriedly, I retraced my steps and tried to circumvent the cemetery on the upper side. I soon found that I was hopelessly lost. At some distance I saw a sinister-looking old man watching me from behind some shrubs—beret on head, pipe in hand. Being my only resource, however, I ventured to ask directions. When I spoke French, it must have touched a magic button, because he quickly opened the gate, smiled, put his arm on my shoulder and most pleasantly gave me directions back to my hotel. I still feel the glow of these encounters with people who were at first strange, distant, and foreboding.

Tucked away securely in my little black book (which

contained all my essential information—addresses, train schedules, important places to see etc.) I kept a picture of my family. On more than one occasion it became a kind of passport to open up strangers or a bridge to my loneliness. The former was the case when I met a Belgian schoolteacher on a bus trip traveling from Perigueux to Angouleme. After seeing the photograph and hearing about my pilgrimage, she gave me an invaluable profile of some little-known churches of merit in central France. It was on her recommendation that I changed my itinerary to visit the little-trafficked church of St. Savin with its multichrome patterned columns supporting a lofty barrel-vaulted ceiling covered with marvelous, though deteriorating, frescoes of major Old Testament stories.

There was one occasion where, through the personal introduction by my former French teacher, I was able to spend some time with a French family who had a summer home on the coast of Brittany. Again, I was warmly taken in, as I introduced them to my family photograph and told them of my interest in French art and architecture. What followed was such a delight—watching a French meal in preparation, the sixty-five year old retired schoolteacher snapping beans into a huge bowl for our dinner while he answered my questions on French history; and the lovely and gracious wife who gathered delicate sea shells and wild flowers for me as we spent an evening watching the sun set over the rocky Breton coast—complete with lighthouse, faded red and blue fishing boats, and a ruined Norman fortress now restored for a rich French businessman.

I must not overlook the sweet old man with the dog. The man gave me a lift from Soissons to Laon while responding with fatherly interest to my adventure. He warned me, kindly, not to accept rides from young men.

My secret was to pick carefully the person with whom I rode (I chose them before they chose me), and especially to tell people what I was doing. Invariably they treated me with deference when I told them I was a professor on a pilgrimage to the churches of France.

Accepting rides from strangers, as I had done on this, my last day in France, was one of the risks born out of both my love for adventure and my proverbial (if not paranoiac) Mormon thrift. The previous day I had spent several of the last few precious hours I had in France trying to get additional funds from the Paris office of American Express. Guilt over having already spent too much money, and the interminable red tape of such offices, led to my abandoning the effort. Instead, I decided to make another adventure of seeing the last of the three major Gothic cathedrals, Rheims, and some adjacent churches—a swing of over 150 miles, with just five dollars in my pocket.

I first purchased a ticket to my immediate destination, Soissons (with its late Romanesque church and an important seat of the Carolingian empire). What followed was the ride with the old man and his dog, and the subsequent trip to Rheims with the family I met in the Laon cathedral parking lot. Now all that remained was the last leg home from Rheims to Paris.

With the small change in my purse I took the bus to the outskirts of Rheims, and from a gas station I hailed a young girl who was en route to Paris in a rickety old Puegeot. She immediately engaged me in conversation, and after very few introductions she asked in French—it sounds peculiar that way— "Have you heard of the Mormon Church?" Surprised, I answered, "Yes, I am a Mormon." We looked at each other and laughed! She had been eager to share her new joy, having been baptized only a month before, she was now on her way to a Youth Conference in Switzerland. Exhausted from the stress which my self-inflicted adventure had brought upon me, I asked permission to take a little catnap and sank into a deep and relaxed slumber.

If simply managing the pilgrimage seemed an overwhelming preoccupation it was largely offset by the tremendous aesthetic gratification of standing in such a place as the narthex of Notre Dame la Grande in Poitiers. I chilled as I saw the morning sun cast a prism of light through stained-glass windows amidst a bustle of morning chores executed by a robed cleric in a matter-of-fact and timeless way. I never wondered or marveled more, nor did I doubt that I was standing in a holy place.

Many of my friends wondered where I found role models for such an adventure. No doubt some of them sifted into my imagination subconsciously from the bright, independent, even arrogant women in the milieu of my Berkeley origins. But my immediate "provocateurs" were historical and literary to some degree. For instance, I had been studying French rather late in life; but so, I found, had Isabella of Castile, who at the age of forty had mastered French and whose daughter, Catherine, was entombed in the marvelous gothic Westminster Abbey after dying an outcast to the capricious court of Henry VIII. Although Isabella's feat was perhaps a minor one, it spoke to me of "today is important; it's the beginning of the rest of your life."

A kind of second mentor, in intellect if not always in deed, was Eleanor of Aquitaine, whose long life reflected the colorful milieu of medieval France. Raised in the sunny, high-spirited, romantic courts of Poitou with its troubadours and tournaments, she had first married the ascetic

Louis VII, Capetian King of France, but actual master of only a small region between Paris and Orleans (the Ile de France). When Louis accepted the call to crusade, brilliantly preached by Abbe Bernard of Blairvaux (whose papal bull promised its standard-bearers indulgences for all past sins), Eleanor insisted on joining him. With many of her "ladies of quality," an innumerable train of baggage-wagons full of clothes, and dressed in the costume of the Queen of the Amazons, she embarked on her crusade-pilgrimage "grand tour."

The crusade was a 12th century disaster, albeit fascinating modern reading. Shortly upon their return, Eleanor, bored with the austere Parisian court, the dismal weather, and the naivety and immaturity of the cloister-driven King Louis, sought the termination of their marriage through papal intercession. Highly prized not only for her lands, but also for her intelligence, grace, and sagacity, she barely escaped the kidnapping attempts of her ardent suitors. It was through her subsequent marriage to Count Henry of Anjou that she became the powerful Plantagenet queen. The union of her lands in Aquitaine with those of the English crown precipitated territorial disputes between her sons (Richard the Lion-heart and John Lackland) and subsequent English monarchs and their French counterparts that lasted almost three centuries.

When people ask me which was my favorite pilgrimage site, I think of Poitiers, where Eleanor and her ladies of court sat in quasi-serious judgment over errant suitors whose demeanor did not measure up to Andreas Capellanus' *Art of Courtly Love,* and I fondly remember the candle I lit at the Church of La Madeleine at Vezelay. I visualize Eleanor, with consummate medieval daring, pageantry, and piety, dressed in her gold-mail Amazon armor accepting the call to crusade. And I imagine the self-effacing, gaunt Abbe' Bernard, the crusade-preacher-visionary, who having exhausted his supply of crosses tore up his own white wool cassock, snipped it into crosses, and distributed them to the newly committed "soldiers of Christ."

My third mentor, I add with no small list of reservations, was the indomitable "Wife of Bath" so sympathetically drawn by Chaucer in the *Canterbury Tales.* Who can fail to delight in her profile, "gap-toothed," "well-wimpled," "broad as a buckler." She had had "five husbands at the church-door" and,

> In company she liked to laugh and chat
> And knew the remedies for love's mischances,
> An art in which she knew the oldest dances.

A regular on the pilgrimage road, she had thrice been to Jerusalem as well as Rome, Bologne, Santiago de Compostella, and Cologne. Although my conveyence was generally the train rather than a donkey, most nights my shoes, too, were "ful moiste" from exhaustive perambulations. I discovered in the "Wife of Bath" a ready example of adventure, mischief, and sheer energy that would later find me pushing myself to the limit.

A typical day might include three stops, such as the day I left Nantes with La Rochelle as my first destination. With a one-hour layover, there was just enough time to streak into and out of churches, towers, bridges, and markets before rushing back to catch the train again for Saintes. At that point there would be a two-hour stop providing time to make the circuit around the Roman arena (three miles by foot from the "gare"), the lovely 10th century abbey (where an early music ensemble was rehearsing for an evening's performance), the museum of antiquities, and back again to the train station and on to Angouleme. Arriving there at supper-time, I bought some snacks and took a twilight tour through the old town before returning, exhausted and "ful moiste," to my hotel just before it got dark. The next morning I splurged and relaxed at a hairdressers' and, in true "Wife of Bath" tradition, shared those salon pleasantries which have for ages been the primary justification for such rituals. Like the "Wife of Bath," no "moths nor mites" ate at my skirts, "For they were used well" and hardly ever off!

These women, Isabella of Castile, Eleanor of Aquitaine, and the "Wife of Bath," were important "provacateurs" for me. If one were to look around, at 19th century profiles of Mormon women, as well as contemporary women, I feel confident that one could find equally stimulating models for those who would pursue both the life of the mind and an occasional flight of fancy that characterized my experience.

Would I advise other women to "break away" from the constraints that an overly protective and/or unimaginative support system would allow? Many Mormon women have already made the break in ways akin to the spirit of my mentors. There are the women who return to college life after years of reigning supreme in a rather manageable "menage" who display a special kind of courage. They face younger, more singly-directed students and perhaps teachers younger than themselves whose criticism and censure of their fledgling efforts are often painful. Other women expose themselves to the business world or to community leadership with equal trepidation and vulnerability. All of these efforts require trading-in a safe, secure, status-quo situation for a questionable and oft-times intimidating exposure to a world of competition and risk.

There is an obvious price to be paid for any such experience. If we do not accept the fact that we must change and adapt, we absolve ourselves of responsibility for growth; we suffer and die spiritually. Either choice is equally hazardous. The ways I tested myself are in no way a paradigm for others but simply the outgrowth of my own personality and needs. As such my experience was my own "pilgrimage and passage" at a point in my life when I needed to prove myself as an individual and as a soon-to-be-released mother. I realized only in retrospect, perhaps, that I needed this "rite of passage," this forging of a personal identity independent of the security dimensions of husband and children, church and community.

If I had a few shaky moments, there came the realization that one cannot have things both ways; one cannot remain comfortable and secure in a predictable and constant world (if there is such a thing), and also experience growth, independence and adventure. That is what the world of the living is all about. Finding that I had within me the resources to make it alone was very satisfying, and the anxious moments were more than compensated for in the afterglow of those few memorable encounters that "defined" me as a person. Moreover, I found that both my strengths and my weaknesses served me well. The strength that set me out with brazen determination to "do or die" resulted in careful planning and study. The weaknesses I have confessed to, dependence and inadequacy, made me genuinely vulnerable and human, eliciting gentle consideration and help from strangers in my need.

There are so few experiences of a lifetime through which we can measure ourselves against a great personal challenge, and few of them are without risks. Who needs them, you ask? I do.

"I am aware
that I am eons from perfection,
but I am, finally,
comfortable with my own identity."
Mary Ellen MacArthur

Cherie Taylor Pedersen

Expanding the Vision

When the women's movement started a number of years ago, I suspect most Mormon women, including me, ignored it. That effort for equality hardly seemed relevant to my life. Rather, it appeared to be a movement undertaken by women who simply did not understand the plan of life and their role in it. Telling myself that I had the answers they seemed to be lacking, I dismissed those strident, demanding voices as unseemly, and certainly unfeminine. After all, was I not equal to man in the eyes of God? As a Mormon woman had I not been told that though my role was different from man's role, I walked beside, not behind him? The restored gospel was a protective barrier for me, and I withdrew behind it, content that it shielded me from the turbulence of a world bent on upsetting the natural order of life as God intended it.

I was naive to feel so insulated. The women's movement has caught up with me—or, more accurately, I have caught up with it. Far from condemning the movement, I now recognize it as instrumental in my personal growth, forcing me to re-evaluate what is important for me as a woman—and what is not. In pursuing that self-knowledge, I have found it necessary to re-examine the concepts pertaining to womanhood that I had once unthinkingly accepted. I have had to enter the elusive world of imagery as I've sought to examine the traditional aspirations and ideals of women within the Church and those of other women whose perspectives are markedly different. Doing so has caused my own perspective to undergo change—difficult even under the best of circumstances, for while change can help steer us toward our goals, it can threaten that which we cherish and obscure that which once was clear.

Slowly, and with much soul-searching, I have come to look upon the movement that has caused such personal upheaval not as a threat, but as a blessing. It has given me room to fulfill chosen roles in my own way and by so doing achieve freedom from unrealistic pressures. This has required a certain juggling of values as I have struggled to weigh the conservative views of woman's role taught by the Church against the more liberal voices of feminists whose perspective, while enticing, lacks vital, gospel-oriented values. The result is my conviction that the goals of both the Church and the women's movement are the same: to help women be the best they can in every aspect of human development. From both the idealistic aura surrounding Mormon womanhood and the hard-eyed assessment of women's needs stressed by the varying voices of the women's movement, I have gradually been able to piece together a realistic pattern for my life.

I grew up in a Mormon home in a part of the country where Mormons were an interesting oddity. My teenage years were spent in the company of friends who neither shared nor fully understood my beliefs, but far from envying my Utah cousins their proximity to church friends and activities, I congratulated myself on having the opportunity for a broader outlook on life than that of Mormons in more insulated communities. However, I became part of such a community when my application to a New England woman's college was turned down, and I applied instead to Brigham Young University.

I looked forward to my experience at a Mormon school in Utah. The prospect of being in an environment where my beliefs and way of life were accepted and understood seemed appealing. I had been different long enough. Ignoring jokes about BYU as the happy hunting ground for girls bent on snaring a returned missionary, I flew west to seek an education. When I left Provo several years later with a diploma, a husband and two babies, I had indeed received an education; along with academics, I had learned what was expected of me as a Mormon woman. Conservative and a traditionalist by nature, I never thought to question the messages I received, both from listening to talks directed at young women and from observing the lives of older women around me.

I learned that the emphasis on marriage at BYU had not been exaggerated. Ten years down the road, I look back incredulously at the scope of some of the activities designed to facilitate that goal. Commonplace were such staples of dormitory life as candle passings (highly romantic engagement ceremonies) and Eternal Marriage Nights featuring hope chest items, bridal gowns and talks on preparing for marriage. Ads for wedding rings and invitations flourished in the student newspaper. Women spent study time making cookies and Christmas stockings and dinners for the men they hoped would take them to the temple and thence to some happily-ever-after wonderland.

The impetus behind these activities stemmed from a concept that taught young women to view their preparation for life largely in terms of preparation for marriage. Under that influence I, too, became so caught up in the quest that I seldom thought about the possibilities of my life outside the framework of marriage. Despite my parents' emphasis on education and personal development, I felt it imperative to graduate wearing not only cap and gown, but a wedding band as well.

My years at BYU, as well as experiences in other Mormon circles after I graduated, introduced me to what I perceived as the "ideal" Mormon woman. To this day I remember a talk given by a woman whom I admired, in which she sketched for us—an audience of BYU coeds—life as envisioned by a starry-eyed young bride aspiring to be little more than a good homemaker and soothing refuge for her husband. Her desire for intellectual development seemed to stem from a desire to be conversant about his interests rather than a need to focus upon her own. Blissfully they would coast through life while raising a large and righteous family. At nineteen, I thought this limited picture was beautiful.

Other images were held up for my inspection, reinforced by countless stories of heroic pioneer predecessors, strong women enduring the hardship and heartbreak of pioneer life without complaint. These were industrious women who became proficient in the many domestic skills necessary for the sustenance of their families, leaving a legacy of thrift and hard work to their daughters. These were spiritual women who relied on the Lord for support of their children and themselves after their husbands were sent away as missionaries to faraway lands.

As I looked around, it seemed that contemporary Mormon women were equally hard-working, capable people who not only oversaw large households with seeming equanimity, but who stocked cupboards with home-canned fruits and vegetables, made quilts and baked bread (always with an extra loaf for a neighbor), and supported husbands in time-consuming church positions. Any excess energy and creativity became channeled into callings in the various auxiliaries. Spare time for more self-serving pursuits seemed a luxury, not a right.

I know the prototype well because I became one. I sought to conform to a way of life I associated with obedience to principles of the gospel. My aims were admirable, but they created enormous pressure to reach a mythological perfection through what I perceived as selflessness. Wasn't that, after all, what the idealistic young bride of that BYU talk had in common with those invincible pioneer women and their equally impressive descendants?

After spending the first six years of our married life in school and a few lean years after that seeking to establish a foothold, my husband and I had finally "made it" in the sense that we were realizing some long-term goals. We had four bright, healthy children and a comfortable home. After surviving the stress of our early years together, our marriage now seemed to be on solid ground. My husband's profession made our lives financially secure; we were both active in the Church—I as a teacher in Relief Society, he as a new bishop. I had everything I considered important in this life—and more.

But far from feeling the satisfaction I thought I should have felt, I was frequently depressed and filled with self-doubt. Rather than rejoicing in the home and children I had been taught to cherish, I found myself feeling more like a slave to their many demands. And although I was proud of my husband and his accomplishments, I began to yearn for my own in areas other than domestic. I tried to suppress these stirrings of discontent, certain that I had no "right" to such feelings. Watching other women cope with unhappy marriages, serious financial strain and poor health, how did I dare *not* be happy? I felt spoiled. I felt ungrateful. Worst of all, I felt that by having needs that seemed to conflict with family and church obligations I somehow fell short of the ideal Mormon womanhood had come to symbolize.

Against this internal discord beat the conterpoint of an ideology fostered by the women's movement: the clarion call to "be" someone, to accomplish in wider fields than those usually afforded to full-time wives and mothers. Dangerous indeed for a woman bred on such maxims as, "No success can compensate for failure in the home," and "The hand that rocks the cradle rules the world."

In an attempt to find a comfortable middle ground, I began to re-examine the concept of selflessness. Is it possible to be *too* selfless, I wondered? Assuming that selflessness can be placed opposite selfishness on a moral spectrum, is it possible that the one extreme is as harmful as the other? At what point does selfishness cease to be a vice? Subjective questions, these, requiring subjective answers. Neither the women's movement nor the Church is equipped to provide them. I decided that each woman must struggle to find her own answers and, because life is never static, answers that seemed satisfactory at one time must necessarily be discarded and new ones found to fit the changing circumstances of a woman's life. Increasingly, the persistent voices of the women's movement contributed to my thinking about that fragile balance between selfishness and selflessness. To many of its opponents the movement teaches selfishness and in some respects that may be a valid observation. However, it helped me realize that those abilities and needs which transcend accustomed roles are deserving also of opportunities for expression without the penalty of guilt.

When our youngest child turned two, the pressure to resolve my conflicts intensified. At no other point in our married life had it seemed so advantageous to have another child. We were able to afford a child. We had established a loving home where principles of the gospel were taught. My husband wanted another child. To deny those advantages to a waiting spirit seemed selfish. What could be more valuable than the raising of a child toward stable, productive adulthood?

Yet, deep within me, I knew I did not really want another baby. Although my years of mothering had brought intense joy, nothing had prepared me for the darker side of motherhood, the one that saps the mental, emotional and physical energy of a woman. Despite the apparent fullness of my life, a void needed to be filled, and I began dwelling on the other satisfactions of my life: music and writing. I began to feel that my sense of self, somehow displaced within the framework of marriage and motherhood, could best be restored if I could seriously develop my literary and musical abilities. To do so would require the time commitments which had eluded me when our children were very young, but I didn't think my need could be ignored any longer.

The guilt I suffered in that wrenching decision was alleviated in part by outside voices that helped me understand that a woman's worth extends to many areas outside the traditional domestic ones. To acknowledge needs that make us unique and to seek to fulfill them is not selfish. It is wisdom born of the understanding that we cannot give to others unless we ourselves are full.

My physician is a woman about my own age whom I

admire tremendously. On my first visit to her, she glanced over my chart and said, "Four children?? How do you manage?" This from a woman with two young children of her own and a growing medical practice!

"How do *you* manage?" I shot back, quickly deciding that this was not the time to tell her that to my Mormon friends ours is a small family. Her juggling act seemed remarkable to me, not just because she was operating on two very demanding planes as a mother and a physician, but because she seemed to be doing so without guilt. Had she been a Mormon woman would she still enjoy that serenity, I wonder? Or would she have to contend with the fear that she was being scrutinized for flaws in her other role?

I have sensed in the turmoil of change fostered by the women's movement a sisterhood nurtured in the sharing of feelings and experiences by women reaching out to one another for answers. We have within the structure of the Church a formal organization of women dedicated to such a sisterhood. It can only fulfill its purpose if its members feel free to reach out to one another without fear of censure. True concern transcends differences and becomes a support system of mutual respect.

The gospel, as I have come to view it, is a celebration of womanhood. It reminds us of the seed of divinity within us and hence our potential for accomplishment of ever-increasing magnitude. So, too, principles embodied in the women's movement can serve as a catalyst to growth by expanding our vision of what women can achieve when given the latitude to tailor traditional roles to individual needs. Accepting the challenges of both has increased my awareness of the multi-faceted nature of my own womanhood and has given me the incentive to narrow the gap between what I am and what I wish to become.

Marlene Payne

Notes from a Water-Worn Stone

I love the feeling of a water-worn stone that just fits my palm. I imagine it as it once was: a jagged shard already a thousand years old. Time flows like water rounding the rough stones of experience. Mercifully, we do not fully remember the work and the suffering of maturing.

I was born third girl to a father who longed for a son, a son to be named Daniel. Later on my father's wish was fulfilled through two sons, but not before I was stamped with an ambition to fulfill his secret dreams, his unlived ambitions.

When I was thirteen, close to the age of Joseph Smith's revelation, I read his biography by his mother, Lucy Mack Smith. I read it in the midst of my own sacred grove of very large trees, passing away the Sunday quiet near a garden of purple and white irises, but my heart was not quiet. My body was ripening and I was irrevocably bidding farewell to all hope of becoming a man. Born and raised in the Church, I mourned at the thought that I would never have the Priesthood and would therefore never produce anything of significance. That year I was given my Patriarchal blessing, part of which said, "All of the souls that have come to this earth have come through the loins of a woman: even Christ himself came through the loins of Mary. In that respect you occupy a very favored position. As a woman you will be acting as a sort of co-creator with your Heavenly Father.'' But I was not to appreciate the wisdom and beauty of this statement until my own children came along.

Solace in this developmental crisis came from another direction, my realization that there is an equality in the Church—an equality of intelligence. I have never accepted the rationalization Brigham Young gave his wife for the patriarchal order in the Church: that man must lead woman because no matter how intelligent the woman, there is always a more intelligent man just ahead of her. The patriarchal order is just that, an order. God and nature are orderly in their work. Existing first as intelligences, we are promised that whatever degree of knowledge we obtain will rise with us in the resurrection. While Mormon culture does not encourage intellectualism, Mormon doctrine does encourage the use of intelligence, the gaining of knowledge. To this end I bent my boundless adolescent energies. I knew easily and without conflict that I would develop a career as well as build a home. I listened to Church talks, hearing what I wanted to hear, and reconstructing the Gospel anew in my life in a pattern consistent with my nature. When I filled out my college applications, I wrote ''pre-medicine'' in the blank for ''intended course of study.'' As I remember it, this decision was made intuitively. Like other major decisions in my life, this one was dictated by unconscious factors. When I was called for an interview as a prospective student in an honors medical program, the benevolent interviewer asked me why I had chosen this field. I answered that I wanted to use my intelligence and I wanted to help people.

But these were not my own reasons. I did not notice it at the time, but my choice was also a compromise, an identification with both parents. My mother is a nurse who takes pride in her career, always working part-time as I grew. My father's doctorate was in microbiology, but medicine had been his first love. Sadly, he had lacked the confidence for medical school. He is not one to share his feelings, (leaving that part of parenting to my mother), so I was both surprised and moved by the red rose he gave me on the day I graduated from medical school.

Premedical and medical training included much that was joyful, but also much that caused suffering. The rational and precise nature of the sciences did not come naturally or pleasantly to me. I longed for music, art, movies, literature, for voices of emotion and intuition. After my second dreary year, I took a year's leave of absence, hoping to mature before I returned. My wise parents kept their fears and doubts to themselves while I worked as a caseworker for the Cook County Department of Public Aid in Chicago. My caseload of alcoholics, schizophrenics, and sociopaths was my first acquaintance with the seamier side of life. At the end of the year I was overjoyed to return to medical school. It was peaceful work caring for patients, wonderful hard work that left me exhausted and deeply satisfied.

While still in undergraduate school at Northwestern, I first saw and fell in love with a proud young man on a motorcycle. My chances of meeting him improved when we both entered medical school—out of 143 students, six were women. Our courtship was leisurely, six years of friendship leading to marriage at the end of our internship. The pace suited me and gave me time to understand and appreciate his sensitive nature.

We both chose to specialize in psychiatry. For me it

was a choice consciously based on superficial reasons. Had I stayed in Chicago, I would have chosen neurology, but my husband was assigned to the Public Health Service in Washington, D.C., and so I chose a residency in psychiatry simply because neurology was not available at the time. This decision also proved intuitively correct. I liked the process of diagnosing and treating physical problems, but I wanted to know my patients as people, deeply and intimately. If their work in therapy succeeded, it would change their lives by healing old wounds. I have always been interested in the unconscious. Before I ever dreamed of psychiatry, my favorite authors were Dostoyevski, Joseph Conrad, James Joyce, D. H. Lawrence. The field suits my nature, and I have never regretted the choice.

But my training, though a fascinating intellectual exercise, was also a time of suffering. I had left medicine, a field in which I had begun to feel competent and entered the unknown field of psychiatry. As a first-year-resident I felt terribly anxious as I sat listening to psychotic patients whom I did not understand and to whom I did not know what to say. Of course experience dulled this anxiety, but psychiatric training is anxiety-provoking and depressing for a different reason: As I began to understand my patients, I began to understand myself also. In fact, I came suddenly face to face with myself, stripped of most illusions. Fortunately, the pain of this knowledge has softened too into a greater acceptance of myself.

Psychiatry has deepened my spirituality; it has made me more humble, more honest, more compassionate, more forgiving, and more active in my attempts to live my religion by serving others. In a curious way, this identity as a psychiatrist has healed the wound I felt as a thirteen-year-old girl. It has fulfilled the masculine side of my nature to have a career and to make my way in the competitive world outside the home. But beyond this, the psychiatrist is a healer, a confessor, a keeper of mysteries; in short, psychiatry is a form of secular priesthood. The spiritual nature of this profession was even more apparent when I began to study Jungian psychology, which is concerned with such mythological themes as the Great Mother.

This theme of the Great Mother hit me with tremendous force. It enlarged my understanding of the nature of femininity to confront the Great Mother with her two faces: the good mother and the terrible mother. The good mother is a source of life, nurturance, creativity, exaltation, while the terrible mother is a suffocating source of madness and death. This dichotomy then is an expression of ambivalence. The images express themselves on a cosmic scale and on a personal scale. (It is great and terrible to be a woman. It is wonderful to be a woman.)

Recognition of ambivalence had come to me from my work with patients long before I studied the Great Mother archetype. Although ambivalence is central to the human psyche, it has been absent from most of my experience in the Church. Even though the Gospel recognizes opposition in all things, Church culture strives to suppress ambivalence, to deal only with the positive, a two-dimensional view. It was a relief to recognize the nature of the ambivalence and to realize that recognition of the negative does not need to destroy the positive.

Another reason that the mythology of the feminine affected me so profoundly was that it is virtually absent in the thoroughly patriarchal scripture and history of the Gospel. Discovery of the enormous extent of the Great Mother archetype in the political, social, religious, and artistic life of varied cultures over a great span of history restored a sense of balance. Of course knowledge of our Heavenly Mother has often comforted me, but we do not hear much about Her.

Although the feminine voice is muted in church history and scripture, the Church does give strong recognition and support to woman as the provider of life, nurturance, and love. To me this is a wonderful role. As a thirteen-year-old child, I was not capable of sensing the joy of this. But after I fell in love with my husband, I found it easy to give to him abundantly and without tally. Since finishing my psychiatric training, I have borne two children and cut my practice to half-time. The role of the Great Mother, then, has become a daily reality, a further source of joy and suffering and the ultimate avenue of my own creativity.

I have also achieved a measure of peace through the attempt to balance masculine and feminine, positive and negative, religious and secular aspects of myself. I have pursued the integration of these opposites in my personal life through the complex interplay of the Gospel, psychiatry, Jungian psychology, my family, and my own intuition. At times, this peace is so strong that it spills over into the simplest acts. I wash dishes and smile to myself. The water flows over my hands, life flows over me, and I am smoothed—a water-worn stone.

Mary Ellen Romney MacArthur

The Paso Robles Rift

On a bright fall day last year I had the joyous experience of driving my daughter Jane to school at Stanford University. I took the long-familiar route up the coast, but we didn't go through Paso Robles as we did in the old days. New freeways now bypass the town, and besides, I no longer need it as a spot to change identities.

Just before we made the trip north, our family was all together at church on Sunday—a rare treat these days, with children ranging in age from twelve to twenty-two. How typically Mormon we look, I thought as we sat in a row; my husband and two sons wore their navy-blue three-piece suits, Tom Junior's a bit frayed and shiny after two hard years of missionary wear, and Matt's roomy and crisp, as befits a new deacon. Our scriptures were piled high in the seat beside me. How proud I felt of my handsome family! A feeling of warmth and love filled me as I saw not only my immediate family, but all the beloved members of our ward family.

But other, more shadowy emotions sometimes lurk in my soul. Is this middle-aged, somewhat overweight Mormon matron really me? Could Tom and I possibly be the parents of these confident young adults? And on a deeper level, what am I doing here anyway? Where is the questing spirit of my youth? This subterranean voice is faint and infrequently heard these days, but my sardonic inner commentator still lives.

I nearly gave away my schizophrenic secret one day this summer when, in a heated discussion over the intrinsic cultural value of rock versus classical music, I loudly proclaimed to my two older offspring that it is easier for me to believe in the divine inspiration of Handel's "Messiah" than in the Joseph Smith story. They were truly shocked! I quickly back-pedaled and said that of course I believed that both were divine but that for most people Handel was easier to accept. Tommy agreed that it was certainly true in Tennessee, anyway, where he had worked so hard to convince people of Joseph Smith's authenticity. But I had revealed a piece of my other self.

I first became vividly aware of my duality while a college student. Going to school in the San Francisco area and living in Los Angeles County meant many long automobile trips up and down the coast, and after a year or so of commuting, I began noticing that I really had developed a "Stanford self" and a "home self." I eventually fell into the habit of marking the pleasant half-way town of Paso Robles as my metamorphosing point; by the time I got there I could feel my values and attitudes shifting. This repeated experience always gave me a curious, unfocused sensation.

It wasn't however, just a case of hometown girl corrupted by worldly university. Things had started going awry for me several years before. I was born a Mormon girl, proud of my pioneer heritage and sure of my identity. Sure, that is, until a stormy adolescence separated me from my peers in what seemed a hopeless estrangement. Emerging from Beehives with a bandelo full of pretty felt awards and an Honor Bee certificate, I was horrified to find that Mutual now seemed to be one endless Tuesday night dance, with everyone knowing how but me. I was urged, begged, and ordered to keep going, but unwilling to let such torture continue, I flatly informed everyone that I was through with Mutual. So I succeeded in growing up Mormon in the 50's without ever being in a roadshow, going to a Gold and Green Ball, or getting a 100-percenter award. I found companionship that suited me better in the pages of books. (I particularly enjoyed reverting to Louisa May Alcott's Jo, though I never could convince myself that she was right in marrying the professor instead of Laurie). Eventually I found friends outside the Church through my orchestra and high school newspaper activities.

My love for music, though frustrated by minimal talent and training, provided great refuge during those years of feeling perennially out of step. Thus it was a blow when our humble ward, trying to stretch itself culturally while also raising some money, displayed its artistic naivete' in an attempt to sponsor a piano recital in our half-finished recreation hall. Our warm, good-hearted bishop, owner of a local body and fender shop, decided to "announce the program" himself, sending me into a paroxysm of embarrassment by mangling nearly every composer's name (*chop*-in as in firewood). Strange that the pain of his gaffe is so real to me still! It instilled in me such a fear of what others might think of our strange folk-ways that years later I still suffer agonies whenever I spot a nonmember in our congregation.

I suppose it was natural to dread and fear going to Brigham Young University, my mother's alma mater. Ever since I heard a popular older girl describe it as "one giant MIA party,'' I knew I would hate it. Though I went through the motions of applying, I put all my eggs in another basket. Older school friends had come back from Stanford raving about its virtues. Though I had never seen it, I applied to Stanford also, despite warnings from my mother, a recent widow, that my going there would be financially impossible without a large scholarship. Friends rejoiced at my being accepted at Stanford, but I blithely took admission for granted, my prayers bent on receiving financial aid. My rationale was this: if the Lord thinks that I should go to the Y, He'll just see to it that I don't get any scholarships! (Little did I suspect then that a similar ''deal'' with the Lord would be made by my daughter some twenty-five years later). Well, Heavenly Father must have a warm spot in His heart for Stanford, because I got not one but two substantial scholarships. (It worked for Jane, too).

I thought that I was a pretty good Mormon when I first went to Palo Alto. For a while I defended ''absolutist'' values in my Western Civ. class, searched for rides to Palo Alto Ward for Sunday School, and attended Deseret Club functions. But I must admit that my real conversion was to Stravinsky, Shakespeare, Donne, history, journalism, San Francisco, and, increasingly, to ''having a good time.'' A food service job (''hashing,'' in the campus lexicon) conflicted with Sunday meeting times; Mormon boys still didn't ask me out. By the end of my sophomore year, my Mormon identity was something that I shed like a coat going up the state, and uncomfortably donned again during summer vacations.

I tried not to be hypocritical. I tried to make my mother understand my feelings. I painfully recall some of those titanic ''discussions,'' one of the most memorable being the issue of prayer. She wanted me to pray for a strengthening of my testimony. I wanted to know what good it was to pray if I wasn't at all sure that I wasn't just talking to myself. Why should I pray for a testimony when I wasn't at all sure it was worth having? My mother was a strong and eloquent woman, and I recall with anguish the tears these debates always brought.

The inevitable followed: I married outside the temple and outside the Church.

Mother tried to tell my new husband something about being married to a Mormon. I squirmed, wishing she wouldn't keep bearing her testimony to him. Tom took it stoically, though; his mother was pretty eccentric too. After all, she preached politics to me, and she found my liberalism as distasteful as Mother did Tom's agnosticism.

Once married and away from home, I could shed my uncomfortable Mormon coat and revert to my liberated, culture-worshipping self. Tom and I revelled in the freedom of marriage, work, and graduate school. Saturday night was for marvelous events in San Francisco, and Sunday was for sleeping in, walking, and studying.

There were some puzzling anomalies in my life, however. When I saw a film with an aerial view of the Salt Lake valley, with temple spires reaching upwards and the Tabernacle Choir singing "Come, Come Ye Saints," I found myself choked with tears, a rare thing for me. During a discussion with a friend about the *Book of Mormon,* I was angered by her implication that it was fraudulent. Those golden plates had always haunted me. I had read the *Book of Mormon* as a young teenager. I knew of its beauty and power, and Alma, Samuel, and other new world prophets were very real individuals to me. It was obvious that Joseph Smith hadn't just "made it all up." One reading of it had converted my Grandmother Anderson in Denmark. The content of the book, I knew, was not false. Did that knowledge then carry with it some obligation?

Tom's army duty on the east coast followed. Though I pictured myself an iconoclast, as a true child of the '50's, I unquestioningly dropped my graduate work and fledgling career to accompany him as a full-time housewife, lonesome, bored, and soon pregnant. Our little town in Pennsylvania made my hometown seem like a cultural metropolis. There was a ward not far away, but I ignored the overtures of the embarrassed home teacher sent to dig us out. I wonder what he thought of us—the silent young engineer-lieutenant and me, the cool inactive member in our bare little apartment, furnished with a picnic table, a day bed, and lots of art posters, books, and records? At the time I thought of "them" as wanting me to fill jobs in a country ward. It never occurred to me then that "they" were just what I needed to survive the long lonely winter of my pregnancy and new motherhood.

The beginning of the melding of my two selves occurred several weeks before Tommy was born. A fellow officer and his wife had just had a baby son, and we were invited to the Lutheran christening ceremony. I listened in angry disbelief. Conceived in sin! Purifying that innocent little bundle? I was once more amazed at my tears and at the strength of my feelings. Surely babies came from God in perfect purity!

Tommy and I came home from the hospital just in time for Easter Sunday. Overwhelmed by the awesome responsibility of parenthood, I yearned, for the first time in years, for my mother's strength and cherishing her frequent loving letters. Long quiet nursing sessions at night led me to contemplation of ideas long buried. I decided that as soon as possible, Tommy and I would go home to California so he could be blessed the proper Mormon way.

I wonder when Tom first saw that he had married a Mormon in Jack's clothing? He had no objections to Tommy's being blessed in my church—he had attended several denominations as a child with no strong feelings pro or con. He wasn't even very surprised when, after being discharged from the service and finding a job with an electronics firm in my hometown, he found himself living with my family while we raised money for a house. It seemed natural for me to go to church on Sunday, and the pattern continued, sporadically, after we found our own house and ward in a nearby town. I was given minor church jobs; occasionally Tom would come along to parties or special programs.

How familiar the above portrait must be! Every ward directory must have several households that fit this description. But the Church is hard to mugwump. I sat for several years, neither in nor out, plagued by my duality, not quite whole. At times I leaped to the Church's defense; at times I criticized it bitterly. I was anxious that our children—by then there were two—go through all the prescribed rituals and lessons, but I was aware that I was not setting a strong home example. By now I could, and did, pray regularly with the children at mealtimes and bedtime although I still avoided personal attempts at spirituality. I began to feel that faith was a talent I had little of, like my lack of ability in mathematics.

I half wish I could report that long fasts and nights of prayer brought me a personal revelation (although I've always thought that they sounded very scary). But instead some things—little things—started happening that were eventually to push me off the fence.

For one, the independent Mormon journal *Dialogue* was born. Furthermore, it was born at Stanford, so it had to be taken seriously. I knew several of the founders, and I had an intense personal interest in the publication from the outset. Some of the articles made a lasting impact on me, notably Victor Cline's "Faith of a Psychologist: A Personal Document" and Richard Poll's description of Liahonas and Iron Rods. For truly the first time in the thirty-plus years of my life, I found that I was not particularly unique or alone in my struggle to unify the intellectual and spiritual sides of my nature. Others, more intellectually sophisticated than I, had fought the same battles and won to the extent that they could function successfully both within and outside the LDS community. Somehow, *Dialogue* seemed to legitimatize us "doubting Thomases" and give us a sense of fellowship we lacked in our individual wards.

Then Tom and I were assigned to a different ward. Our new ward was highly tolerant of diversity and we were eagerly welcomed both socially and ecclesiastically. Our talents were valued, we were both put to work, and for the first time we developed a warm circle of Mormon friends.

In one of the letters Mother had sent me around the time of Tommy's birth, she had begged me to get out my *Book of Mormon* and reread Alma's brilliant discourse on the cultivation of faith. On several occasions since then I had read and thought about my feelings for the *Book of Mormon* and my demonstrated belief in the pre-existence. Could they be the seeds that Alma was talking about? Did I now "desire to believe" enough to nurture the seeds' growth? I recalled the philosophy of William James, by far the most significant to me when studying ethical systems in my undergraduate days. I was increasingly acting as though I believed, and as James and the prophet Alma both predicted, such "acting" was leading to increased belief. Was I prepared to live up to the consequences? It still scared me; half-in, uncomfortable as it was, was much less demanding than wholly in.

Our children (now numbering three) were growing up as committed Latter-day Saints, thanks, I am sure, to the powerful teachers and youth leaders in our beloved ward. Tommy and Jane were asking pointed questions about transgressions from the letter of the law and, good father that he has always been, my husband found himself obligated to set a good example, Mormon-style. When Tommy became a deacon, of course we all attended sacrament meeting to support him. And as an interested Scout father, Tom began first going on overnight trips, and then on to the big Sierra backpacking expeditions with the troop.

There was never any question about whether Tommy would serve a mission. He belonged to a large, active priests quorum where all the boys planned missions. We seemed to take it for granted that Tom would support him, financially and morally, as he had throughout all Tommy's Scout and priesthood assignments.

It was a dear friend, ex-bishop, backpacking buddy, Stanford-educated lawyer, who saw better than we did what was happening. He arrived on our doorstep (albeit with shaking knees, he later admitted) to give my husband "the lessons." The good seeds, dormant for so long, had enlarged our souls and had become delicious to us. And so it was that, on his 19th birthday, Good Friday 1978, my son Thomas Romney MacArthur baptized my husband Thomas Douglas MacArthur, and I found myself in the bosom of the Church. Tommy was serving his mission in Tennessee when the rest of us were sealed in the Los Angeles Temple.

That spring a poignant realization brought my two selves into near synchronism. My mother, ill for years, survived just long enough to be with us in the temple. She had suffered a stroke and was living with us when the time came for our endowments. We had some precious long talks together during that time, and I saw what she had tried to conceal and I had missed for so long: that my doubts, skepticism, intellectual inclinations, and struggles for personal faith closely paralleled her own. It was no accident that she too had been an early *Dialogue* supporter and contributor! The Paso Robles rift between Stanford and my mother's values had existed mostly in my own faulty perception.

I've learned since what Jane and my mother seem to have always instinctively known: that it is perfectly possible to be considered a liberal, intellectual feminist at church and a religious, conservative "square" in the world and still be accepted in both spheres. I still tend to ruffle my feathers at too much emphasis on unthinking obedience, and my ward friends are accustomed to—in fact *expect* me to—play the role of devil's advocate in any good discussion. Our home is still filled with music, books, and art and some furniture, and I am aware that I am eons from perfection. But I am, finally, comfortable with my own identity.

By the time Jane entered Stanford and we made the trip up Route 101 together, it was the same complex, cranky, conscientious Mary Ellen who left Pasadena and arrived in Palo Alto. As I left Jane at the familiar vine-encrusted dormitory, the possibility of new rifts—between new generation women and older values—seemed a scary possibility. But overriding the worry was a powerful sense of pride and continuity. Jane, like her grandmother in most ways, is up to the challenge.

Elizabeth O. Wach

Have a Good Time

"Did you have a good time?" he asked as he signed my recommend. What beautiful penmanship! He put a lovely "S" on Simon and a very ornate "P" on Peter. I accepted my recommend from this heavenly gatekeeper and started to float through the pearly gates. That watchful being stopped me to ask, "Did you enjoy yourself?"

"Oh?" I murmured, securely tucking the recommend into the pocket of my home-sewn dress accented with smocking and pearls, next to my hand-embroidered, hand-monogrammed handkerchief. "Let's skip the small talk, the supernatural formalities and get to thc important things in afterlife—I'm on my way to my first immortal meeting!"

But the gatekeeper was in no hurry. He put his featherlight hand on my arm with the same warm touch he had used when he helped me up that last step and shook my hand in welcome. Time probably meant nothing to him; he had all day—maybe eons—to talk. This relaxed pace bothered me. A minute not used constructively is a minute wasted, I used to tell my kids back on earth. Maybe I should tell St. Peter that, too! After all, the idle mind, heart, hands—you name it—the idle anything is the devil's workshop! Wasn't that true up here, too?

Just as I was about to wrench myself from his fragile grip, he smiled, motioned me to a marble seat nearby and gently helped me sit down. The two inches of crocheted ruffle on the bottom of my dress brushed against the ground—if you can call gleaming crystal "ground," but I didn't worry. It wouldn't get dirty here, and if by any earthly (heavenly?) chance it should, I knew of twenty-seven different ways to remove stains, using items that should be included in every well-organized Mormon home storage. He smiled, but I sighed when he asked again, "Did you have a good time?"

"On earth? When? Where exactly—chapter and verse—do you mean?" I do everything by the handbook. When in doubt, read the manual!

"To start with, did you ever enjoy a sunrise?"

"Sunrise? Let me tell you about sunrises! I should know because for a good twenty years of my life I got up before the sun did—sometimes when it was still pitch black—at 5 A.M. Mormon Standard Time (that's really 5:07 to 5:12 by anyone else's mortal clock) and I jogged! I'd go three miles on the level, two miles up and two down that hill by the grade school where I did volunteer work for the PTA for all those years the children went there. I'd sprint the last mile back home, have a quick shower with the rose-glycerine soap I had made in Relief Society, and then I'd read the scriptures!"

"Scriptures, sister? Which did you enjoy most?"

"I read them all, and on a well-planned schedule, too. Every morning for twenty minutes without fail, even on the way to the hospital to have a baby—DeVerla, I believe it was—I read those scriptures. I studied the standard works, dividing the time according to their length. My planned twenty minutes called for:

12 minutes of the *Bible*
5 minutes of the *Book of Mormon*
2 minutes of the *Doctrine and Covenants*
½ minute of the *Pearl of Great Price*

and I didn't neglect current "scripture." I read

½ minute of the message of the First Presidency that appeared in the *Ensign* each month. Thanks to my

20 minutes a day, I read and reread the scriptures all right!"

St. Peter frowned slightly. "That schedule doesn't leave much time for meditation, prayer, or pondering on the word of the Lord. Can you enjoy scripture by *reading* only?"

"Well, the Lord said to seek knowledge out of the best books, and what could be better than the standard works and the *Ensign*?"

"Did you enjoy the *Ensign*?"

"I read it and the *New Era* and the *Friend* every month. I took them even when I no longer had children or teenagers. They are super magazines—all except for the poems and the fiction. You see, I never would read anything that wasn't true! I didn't miss an issue of the Church magazines. In fact, we didn't subscribe to anything else in *my* household! Church books and magazines were all we read!"

The gatekeeper looked away, mumbling something about Shakespeare, politics, Thornton Wilder, Robert Frost, economics, foreign languages, Tolstoy and Poe. I wrinkled my forehead. Had he—of all people—expected me to waste time on worldly, non-Mormon trash? Tsk!

In a few seconds (minutes? Heavenly time is hard to calculate) he asked, "Did you enjoy attending the Temple?"

"Ah, the Temple! I told my bishop I'd go twelve times a year, and since I lived in Salt Lake City—wouldn't live anywhere except in Zion where the Church is—I could easily attend the Temple. So, I took four days out of every January and did my assignment the right way—three sessions a day, and it was done! But—pardon my pride—I lengthened my stride like the prophet said we should and did fourteen sessions. That's two more than I promised the bishop at tithing settlement!"

"Did you enjoy the blessings of paying tithing?"

"I never missed a month of paying my ten per cent. I wish we had a coin smaller than a penny on earth because sometimes I'd owe the Lord—uh—something like $9.73½ cents. We surely could have used a new coin down there. Anyway, I always paid *exactly* and never missed. I paid my fast offerings, too. I figured what I spent for two good meals right down to the homemade butter on the homemade bread that I made from my home-ground wheat. I never wanted to cheat the Lord. To be on the safe side, once in a while I'd give to the missionary fund even if I didn't know any of the missionaries! And when the bishop asked us what we felt we could give to the budget, we told him we'd be proud to pay $10 a month. And we did, too, right on time. One month I nearly forgot and had to send the money air mail because we were vacationing—our only vacation—in Tahiti at the time."

"Tahiti? Did you enjoy that beautiful island?"

"Not really. It was too hot, humid, and full of foreigners. I was glad to get back to Salt Lake where I could understand the language! I don't know why the missionaries are all so thrilled to receive calls to foreign countries! After our children were raised, my husband and I went on a mission to Louisiana.''

''Speaking of missionaries, sister, did you enjoy your mission? Good Cajun cooking in Louisiana—shrimp gumbo, rice, crawfish . . .''

''We never ate any of that stuff—too much like the cooking in a foreign country. Besides, we were too busy teaching. They didn't know some of our favorite Church songs, so we taught them ''O Ye Mountains High,'' ''Utah, We Love Thee,'' and ''Our Mountain Home So Dear.'' We really made that branch sing!''

''Did you enjoy the people in Louisiana?''

''The people? We did everything for them! Before we came, nobody knew how to keep the minutes, take rolls, or keep statistics. We did all the clerk's duties, played the piano, conducted the meetings, taught all the lessons, did home teaching and visiting teaching. I worry about them even today and wonder who is doing all those jobs since we left them. When I was a girl, my bishop approached me about a mission, too, but I never had a mission as one of my goals. If I had gone on a mission, I probably would never have had the chance to get married and raise a family.''

''Did you enjoy your family, sister?''

''I have the greatest family—took a lot of work and grim determination, but they are fine children—four girls and three boys! We had family prayer morning and night, no matter what! Once when our son LaDar was on the football team, his coach came to get him for something one night, but we made Coach wait in the hall until we finished family prayer.''

''Didn't you invite him to sit down—or to join you?''

''No. Since he wasn't a family member, we knew he wouldn't fit in. And besides, the football coach wasn't even a Mormon—then.''

''He was baptized later?''

''Yes. I think one of the boys who sat on the bench the year that LaDar was an all-state wide receiver invited Coach and his family to a family home evening. It wasn't long until Coach listened to the missionaries and joined the Church.''

''Did you enjoy family home evenings?''

''I made a chart, month by month—laminated it to keep it nice and clean—and everyone took turns praying, choosing songs and helping make dessert. When our oldest daughter Shaleen was to be initiated into the National Honor Society on a Monday night, we made her stay home rather than miss a family home evening. I'm proud to say *I* taught my children not to miss family night!''

''Did your children enjoy giving the lessons?''

''Oh, their dad gave the lessons. I think children should respect the head of the house. My husband always presented the lessons, starting with number one in the manual and going straight through to the end.''

St. Peter looked down at his fisherman's arms, muscular and strong, and frowned. ''No *activities* on Monday? With the combined meeting schedule on the Sabbath, you could have lessons that evening. On Monday go to a ball game, a movie, a National Honor Society initiation. Did you love your family?''

''Of course I did!''

''Did you enjoy telling them that you loved them?''

''Well, we weren't big on public displays of affection, but they knew I loved each and every one of them—I didn't have to *tell* them. I helped them set goals, plan their days, their school, their jobs, their mates—I gave them guidance and advice as well as allowances and balanced meals. And I drove them to parties, programs, activities, basketball games . . ."

"Did you enjoy watching your children in a program or a game?"

"I didn't watch often, but I made sure they had a ride home. Relief Society kept me busy—I was president for five years—so I would drop the kids off at their practices or games and use the time to prepare a lesson or take a meal to a sick member-neighbor."

"Member-neighbor?"

"Yes, we looked after the sick and the afflicted!"

"Non-members, too?"

"We weren't very well acquainted with non-members and didn't know if they were sick or not. Earth life went so fast that it was all we could do to help members, let alone non-members!"

St. Peter smoothed his long beard but didn't say much. I guess he wouldn't know about modern times. The Church today—or when I was on earth last—was so much more complex than when he had lived years ago. Fortunately, we had modern inventions to help us—television broadcasts of Conference, for one thing. And computers, microfilms for genealogy records—He must have read my thoughts, for he smiled again.

"Did you enjoy meeting your ancestors when you did your four generation family group sheets?" he asked.

"Family group sheets? Oh, you mean genealogy! The work for my ancestors has all been done—my great-aunt Alfaretta did it! There was nothing left for me to do—one line goes all the way back to Adam!"

"And the four generation sheets?"

"Hmmmm . . . I think . . . yes, I'm pretty sure my brother sent them in."

"You didn't make *certain* they were complete? Accurate?"

"Well, St. Peter, genealogy is such a dead subject (good pun, eh?) and you wouldn't need to worry if you had a great-aunt like I had! Alfaretta was really a worker who must have spent her last fifteen years living at the genealogy library. Once she told us it was thrilling to find names and places of our family. Because of all the time and effort she spent searching for them, she knew them and their personalities. She said that she loved them. When she died she wanted to meet her ancestors immediately!"

"Would you enjoy meeting your ancestors? You'll have an eternity to talk to them!"

I stared at the lace slippers on my feet. How do you tell someone that you really don't want to talk to ancestors because you've been so busy with important things that you've forgotten unessential small talk and chit chat? I cleared my throat. "I really don't know any of them too well—they probably aren't interested in me either."

"Not even great-aunt Alfaretta? Want to talk to her?"

"Alfaretta's been dead almost five years now—I haven't seen her in—oh, must be ten, eleven years. I don't know what we'd talk about. She won't remember *anything* about earth!"

"What will *you* remember? Family trips to the coast? Yellowstone? Lake Powell?"

"We didn't travel very often. I never felt right about attending strange wards or missing Primary or Relief Society. One hundred percent attendance was my goal!"

"Did you enjoy the association with the women? Maybe stay after meetings and exchange ideas? Or go to a play or a luncheon with them?''

''I wasn't much for staying after meetings—I usually had another meeting to attend, or I had to load up my car with visual aids or decorations. I had the best table decorations for Relief Society luncheons in the whole ward—lots of silk flowers!''

''Did you enjoy flowers? Autumn leaves? Did you enjoy sunsets? Waterfalls? Deserts? Pine trees? Rainbows?''

''But—''

''Did you enjoy toasting marshmallows over a campfire? Ice skating with your children? Swapping jokes with the grand-kids?''

''Did you enjoy the symphony? Pizza? Melodramas? A pet dog? Legislative sessions? Boxing matches? Valentines?''

''Well—''

''Did you enjoy the zoo? Watermelon? Testimony meeting? Summertime? A good novel? Lemonade? Disneyland? Your next-door neighbor?''

''Did you enjoy—''

''STOP!!'' I screamed as I jumped up, nearly tripping on the hem of my white gown. How had this kind saint with the understanding eyes and gentle touch changed into a ferocious grand inquisitor? I struggled to calm my earthly temper. ''Why do you keep asking over and over 'Did you enjoy' when we talk about earth? What do you mean? Were we supposed to *enjoy* life?''

''Exactly! Sister, that's the purpose of our mortal existence—to enjoy everything good and great and wonderful on earth.''

Peter's powerful voice dissolved into a series of

diminishing echoes in the expanse of space. For a long time—years by earthly clocks—we sat there without saying another word. It takes time—and silence—to understand and accept. He put his arm around my shoulders as I wiped away my tears. I reached into my pocket.

"Could you hold this recommend for me for a while? I guess I'm not ready for the afterlife—yet. May I have a little more time on earth, please? I've forgotten something important."

"Of course, sister. We'll keep your recommend safe for your return." He smiled, his eyes warm, his handshake strong and encouraging. My lace slippers silent on the crystal floor, I walked from the marble bench and paused at the edge of mortality. He waved at me as I stepped away.

"Have a good time, sister. Enjoy yourself!"

"I will! This time I truly will."

Loretta Randall Sharp

Saturday Voice— Sunday Burning

Hands are placed on my head, I am told to receive the Holy Ghost, and I am expected then to recognize the still, small voice, understand burning confirmations, take affront at dark feelings, and interpret dreams and visions. True, I am promised that I will receive no general revelation for the Church and no insight contrary to established doctrine. I can, moreover, always test my understanding against the teachings of the Brethren. Such generalizations steady me and provide hope, but the difference between assurance and application remains great. Particular stewardship demands particular assistance. I invest little energy in considering the growth of the Church in Asia or the low standard of living among the saints in Central America. And my grapplings with doctrinal intricacies occur usually when preparing a talk for sacrament meeting or a lesson for family home evening. I am a single parent, the mother of a daughter attending college, a teacher in a fine arts boarding school, an aunt raising a teenage nephew, and a writer. My stewardship means that I invest energy and time wondering how to serve as a surrogate parent to sixty students a day, how to once and for all teach my nephew the difference between a sentence and a fragment, how to persuade my daughter that she must make it through one more semester of education courses if she's to become an elementary school teacher, how to prepare my Sunday School lesson, or how to end a poem. In short, I, like most Church members, require the gifts of the Spirit to help me work through the ordinary circumstances of an ordinary life.

Because the process of receiving and interpreting revelation is so personal and so often confusing and because it requires unremitting discipline, some members of the Church forego the experience. Others choose to trust leaders and to govern their lives according to the generalizations and specifics offered either by the general leadership of the Church or by the immediate leadership in wards and stakes. Still others forego the revelatory process altogether when they become frightened by the failure of some Church members.

Because our lives touch one another so closely, those failures are always too apparent. In the Traverse City Branch, I watched two of our most devoted members forfeit church participation because of revelatory experience. Both were given to much prayer, much fasting, much genuine dependence on the Savior and the Father. One felt repeatedly confirmed in the need to hold together a weak marriage, so she daily worked harder at being good, thinking that if she could only perfect herself, she could then withstand and correct the imperfections of her circumstance. As she increased the regimen of faithful behaviors, she received insights for herself, for her family, and for others—sometimes true and helpful, sometimes not.

An example of the latter kind occurred one Fast Sunday when she darted from her row to mine and asked that I record in shorthand the blessing about to be given to the next baby. She felt prompted to understand that because this was an unusual child, the blessing must be recorded. Startled, I scratched through my purse for a pen and recorded what seemed to be a typical father's blessing. At the end of the meeting, I learned that the parents themselves had taped the blessing on cassette. This small example suggested that the discipline the woman had set for herself was too hard, the results unsettling and inconsistent. Branch members pulled away from her, especially as she received more and more revelations for them. In time the woman's husband left, her children were given to others to raise, and she drifted from church participation.

Another member in this same branch was the finest home teacher I've ever seen. Because he knew without being told the needs of those families assigned him, he provided a telling example of the way the priesthood works when stewardship is honored. He, like the woman previously mentioned, spent hours, then days, in prayer and fasting, working ever harder at receiving the gifts of the Spirit. And he received revelation after revelation. Finally, however, he grew almost autonomous, accepting only those doctrines and ordinances for which he received spiritual confirmation at the moment. His awareness of evil spirits increased; to exorcise them, he beat first his wife, then the infant children who distracted him from his prayers and meditation.

Such instances are not confined to inexperienced branches of the church. In 1979-80, on a sabbatical leave in Provo, Utah, I met in my thriving and well-run ward a sister deeply committed to living a life guided by the Spirit. The results of her devotion were miraculous healings, repeated insights, and constant awareness of the evil and

constant awareness of the evil and good forces at work in her life and the lives around her. The ward members responded to her the way people always do to those floating two inches above the ground—sometimes bewildered, sometimes condescending, always awkward.

What can I learn from these struggles with the Holy Ghost? Surely not that I am exempt from the effort. No church member may refrain from the revelatory moment because of possible mishap. The faithful are, in fact, expected to know the Savior personally. Joseph Smith amended the seventh chapter of Matthew to indicate that Christ will rebuke those who accomplish miracles in his name but who, nonetheless, do not know Him. It would appear that well-intended persons involved in good works are not faulted because Christ does not know them but rather because "Ye never knew me."[1]

While literature seldom focuses on methods for knowing the Savior, many stories center on moments of truth. In the preface to *Winesburg, Ohio,* an old man dreams and then theorizes that in the beginning "each truth was a composite of a great many vague thoughts."[2] People snatched up the truths. The strong ones snatched up many. The old man concludes: ". . . the moment one of the people took one of the truths to himself, called it his truth, and tried to live his life by it, he became a grotesque and the truth he embraced became a falsehood."[3] The community, Winesburg, reflected collective truth—the individuals who lived by single truths were, however, crippled or grotesque.

We may not yet be Zion, but neither are we to be Winesburg, and I must learn to receive individual truth without becoming crippled in the process. This I can do if I remember that such truth (whether its origin be the still, small voice, the burning confirmation, the dream, the sudden flash, or the unexpected insight) is *limited* and *transient*. It is limited because while it may reflect a general principle, it occurs in response to a specific circumstance; it is transient because it will be modified by other truths as circumstances change.

I once experienced difficulty with someone who had caused me offense, and I'd spent several years trying to resolve the problem. The harder I tried, however, the worse things became. One Saturday after trying and failing again, I decided to walk home from work and pray for a new way of forgiving, a new way of trying. I had not walked far when I heard the still, small voice: "He cannot be forgiven until he repents." I knew instantly that I would never again focus on that particular matter, and my relief was total. That evening, however, when the relief seemed no longer novel, I wondered why I had worried so long, tried too hard for so many years. Why had I never understood that repentance was prerequisite to forgiveness?

The next day was stake conference, and I dutifully listened throughout the meeting. Then our stake president began the concluding talk. His subject: D&C 64:10, "I, the Lord, will forgive whom I will forgive, but of you it is required to forgive all men." My listening expanded from the dutiful to the truly attentive. I felt a burning confirmation of his words as he spoke emphatically to the point that we must forgive others whether they repent or not.

So what to do? On Saturday I'd learned one thing, on Sunday its opposite. Bewildered though I was, I did not tell the stake president he had just delivered twenty minutes of false doctrine. But neither did the Sunday burning cancel the Saturday voice. I prayed, and I waited.

And it was several weeks before I understood—this time neither with the aid of the still, small voice nor with a burning confirmation—but with an enormous calm that stilled my unease. The principle of forgiveness is eternal; that is to say, it is God's. But that same Father guides individual lives. His vision surpasses ours, and He will let us know how to expend effort. The Saturday voice was right for that instance, that time, that place. The Sunday truth remains true and governing. Were I to be assigned a talk on forgiveness, I'd speak to D&C 64:10; I'd follow Sunday's confirmation. But I will continue to rely on the Saturday voice to help me personally apply the principles, moment by moment.

When I faced an altogether different difficulty with someone who caused an altogether different offense several years later, I learned again the limits and the transience of individual revelation. Again I supposed myself clearly in the right, the other person clearly wrong. Then in an October moment, I happened to be especially sensitive to the small creatures in our woods, realizing how shy and frightened they were. On that same day, I spent time with young students and was aware that they, too, were shy and frightened. That evening I prayed warm thanks for perceiving so much beauty, and I asked to be sensitive to all shy and frightened beings about me. Images passed before my closed eyes. Somewhere after the chipmunks and squirrels and between the ninth and tenth graders came the face of the person with whom I'd recently felt a difference.

I realized then that I had not understood the vulnerability of the person who had caused me pain. After the tutelage of prayer and a simple truth, I became softer in the relationship, more allowing; I had seen an aspect of one of our Father's children that I had not previously understood—not an entire personality to be sure, just a facet, as much as I was willing or perhaps prepared to bear. And the following Sunday in General Conference, Elder Gordon B. Hinckley gave a talk on forgiveness, counseling that there is no peace in harboring old grudges and pleading with the saints to bind up the wounds "caused by cutting words, by stubbornly cultivated grievances."[4] I listened, knowing that I had not yet learned all the theory of forgiveness, nor had I yet mastered the practice.

Each understanding, each truth I receive is valid and helpful to me; each is also limited and transient. I receive as much truth on any given matter as I am perfected to hear. The truths others acquire differ from mine—they may reflect different principles or they may reflect the same principles in different ways.

My awareness that each of us must learn to accommodate differences comfortably was underscored at a meeting in Provo where a guest speaker discussed the moment she had received the now better-known-than-it-should-be insight that "patriarchy is a sham." As she explained her preparation for that moment, I felt no quarrel—either with the inception of the statement or the statement itself. What I felt was relief that I had not had to work that one out. But, oh, the fireworks that statement ignited, the repercussions of that individual awareness for her and for the Church! That so much grief was unnecessary became painfully, ludicrously apparent to me shortly thereafter at the Women's Conference at Brigham Young University. There I listened to the needs-to-be-better-known address, "Patriarchy and Matriarchy," where Hugh Nibley observed calmly, "There is no patriarchy or matriarchy in the Garden."[5] In discussing the world after the fall, he continued his observations:

> All have fallen but how *far* we fall depends on us . . . Central to the drama was a never-ending tension and conflict between the matriarchal and patriarchal orders, both of which were perversions. Each has its particular brand of corruption . . . matriarchy and patriarchy *must* always be mortal enemies. Why? Because of the last part of the word, the *-archy.* In Bailly's dictionary, the first definition given for the word *-arche* is "beginning, specifically the origin of a quarrel or a 'murder' "; the second definition is "command, power, authority," which is what the quarrel is about. *-Archy* means always to be first in order, whether in time or eminence; the point is that there can only be *one* first. To be first is Satan's first principle.[6]

The word, "sham," pales beside "Gog" when Nibley concludes his talk:

> So one must choose between Patriarchy and Matriarchy until the Zion of God is truly established upon the earth. It is that old Devil's Dilemma, in which we are asked to take sides with Gog or Magog as his means of decoying us away from our true dedication to that celestial order established in the beginning.[7]

No fireworks. No television cameras, no reporters, no church courts. Just a talk and then an essay published in *Blueprints for Living, Perspectives for Latter-day Saint Women,* with a foreword by President Spencer W. Kimball. And the title does not read "*The* Perspective"—it suggests instead that we live with and from multiple perspectives.

Perspective for one. Apostasy for another. No less painful if the perspective unsettles more than the apostasy. Winesburg is never far from us—nor the Pogo realization: "I have seen the enemy—and he is us."

A while ago, a friend said she thought I would like an article by one of the Brethren that gave her particular understanding about the way married partners are essential to each other's resurrection. I replied dubiously, "Maybe—but he's not my favorite General Authority." She knew I thought too many of his speeches conveyed condescension towards women.

But I read the article and smiled. I knew so well where she was in the workings of her marriage that I could respond, "I see what you've understood, but had I not read with your eyes, I would have missed the insights because of the references to women." She then read the article again, smiling at every touchy reference she had previously missed. Had we shared the reading with a third person we knew well, one strong in his or her own right and shaped by unique experience and individual revelation, each of us would have received the article with three different and simultaneous understandings.

Christ's church does not exist in the abstract. The members constitute the Church, but the Savior cannot claim us until we function as a unified whole. The community single to the glory of God is not, however, a community of clones. I have learned that I need not fear diverse insights if I sustain myself and others as children of heavenly parents and sustain those parents as parents. Fortunately, they sustain themselves as our parents even when we slip. I believe we slip most when we fear the price involved in knowing them.

The fact is that we do need one another. There is not

time, not within the confines of mortal time at least, for us to learn everything ourselves. But neither must we settle for the single truth because, after all, we recognize the still, small voice, understand burning confirmations, take affront at dark feelings, and interpret dreams and visions. If we allow ourselves instruction from heavenly beings in different ways, and if we then celebrate rather than fear differences in one another, we will do as our Heavenly Father commands: we will become one, we will receive the Holy Ghost.

---

[1]*Joseph Smith's New Translation of the Bible,* Herald Publishing House (Independence, Mo., 1970), p. 252.

[2]*Winesburg, Ohio,* Sherwood Anderson, Viking Press (New York, 1967), Preface, p. 25.

[3]*Ibid.*

[4]"Of You It Is Required To Forgive," Elder Gordon B. Hinckley, General Conference, October, 1980, *Ensign,* November, 1980, p. 63.

[5]"Patriarchy and Matriarchy," Hugh Nibley, *Blueprints for Living, Perspectives for Latter-day Saint Women,* Brigham Young University Press (Provo, Utah, 1980), p. 48.

[6]*Ibid,* pp. 48–49.

[7]*Ibid,* p. 61.

About the Authors

Phyllis Nelson Barber has published in *Utah Holiday, The Friend* and in *Exponent II.* She has won several awards for her writing, among them the Andy Adams Prize for short fiction sponsored by the University of Utah, the Sigma Delta Chi Professional Journalism Award, and Honorable Mention in the Utah Fine Arts literary contest of 1981 in the Feature Article Division. A professional musician, Phyllis is married to David Barber. Their three sons Christopher, Jeremy and Bradley are learning to be musicians. The Barbers live in Salt Lake City.

Maureen Ursenbach Beecher is Associate Professor of English and Research Historian with the Joseph Fielding Smith Institute for Church History at Brigham Young University. She has written several studies on the history of Mormon women and is currently preparing three volumes on Eliza R. Snow. The essay in this collection won second prize in Dialogue's "Mormon Women Speak" contest. She is married to Dale Beecher and is the mother of Daniel and Bronwen.

Ann Edwards-Cannon has a BA in English from BYU and is now working on her Master's degree. She has published many articles and stories in *Dialogue, Co-Ed, Sunstone, Exponent II, The Friend, Network, The New Era* and *'Teen Magazine.* She is married to Ken Cannon.

Judith Rasmussen Dushku is Assistant Professor of Government at Suffolk University in Boston. Her special interests are comparative politics and international law. She is involved in issues and organization on third world politics. Judy is involved in her community in school, day care, and women's issues. She has three sons and a daughter and is divorced. She loves music—her "standard church job" is ward choir director. She contributed essays in *Mormon Sisters* and in *Sister Saints.* Her essay won first place in the "Mormon Women Speak" contest.

Gladys Clark Farmer served a mission to France, graduated from BYU with a BS Degree and from the University of Denver with an MA. She is the author of the popular missionary novel, *Elders and Sisters.* Gladys is a musician, she teaches part-time in the English Department at BYU and is coach of the BYU "College Bowl" team. She and her husband, James, are the parents of five.

Rubina Rivers Forester earned her BA at BYU and has taught eleven years in the public schools of Samoa, Hawaii and Utah. Some of her work has appeared in *Kula Manu, Ka Po'E O Laie, Mana,* the *Ensign* and the *Church News.* She and her husband Leslie L. Forester are the parents of six children. Rubina loves to sew, write and read. She is a science fiction fan who eagerly awaits an "encounter of the third kind."

Elinor Godfrey Hyde has published in *Exponent II, The Deseret News,* the *Ensign, Spectrum, New Era, Real Estate West of Denver* and *The Prospector.* She has received several writing awards from the League of Utah Writers, of which she is president of the Salt Lake Chapter. She has awards from the Utah Poetry Society and the National League of American Pen Women. She is in real estate and is a commercial sales representative for Fernwood Candies. Elinor is married to Alan A. Hyde and is the mother of six children.

Jerrie Wirkus Hurd has a BA from the University of Colorado and an MFA in Creative Writing from the University of Oregon. Her work has appeared in *Dialogue, Exponent II,* other women's magazines, in-flight magazines and the *Ensign.* She has won first place for fiction in the writing contest sponsored by *Literature and Belief,* a new literary journal at Brigham Young University. The essay in this collection won Honorable Mention in the "Mormon Women Speak" contest. Jerrie, her husband Jon, their two sons and pets live in Oregon. She enjoys photography, needlepoint, cooking and jogging.

Jean Wadsworth Johnson teaches Seminary and Gospel Doctrine and serves as counselor in the Young Women's Organization. She joined the church with her family in 1957 and her son now serves as her bishop in the midwest. She is the mother of six children all active in the church.

Edna Bryant Laney received her BA degree from BYU in 1981 at the age of 61. She is a worker in the Washington, D.C. temple and the mother of seven children—all BYU graduates with the exception of the youngest who is attending BYU. She has traveled extensively having visited China, Russia, Japan, most European and South American countries. She is interested in quilt making and served as vice-president of the National Quilting Association. Her essay in this collection won Third Prize in the "Mormon Women Speak" contest. She wrote "Faithful Felicia," a children's operetta which was performed extensively in church and civic groups in the Washington, D.C. area. At present she is writing a book.

Mary Ellen Romney MacArthur is an English and Journalism teacher in Pasadena, Ca. After graduating from Stanford, she studied at Berkeley and at Los Angeles State. She is married to Thomas MacArthur and they are the parents of three. She is an avid reader, avid Stanford fan, avid in her appreciation of her children's musical efforts. Her favorite hobby is traveling. She serves as the gifted/talented coordinator at the secondary level in her state's education program. Mary Ellen recently renewed her studies towards a Master's Degree at California State University at Los Angeles.

Myrna Dee Schlegel Marler is the mother of six boys. She loves writing, the beach, jogging, and is working on a degree in English. Her most recent publication is a scholarly paper titled ''Hamlet's Several Dilemmas: Some Answers'' in the *Alpha Chi Recorder,* a publication of the National Honor Society. Myrna is married to Michael G. Marler.

Carol Clark Ottesen has degrees in English and Music from BYU and from CSU. She is presently working toward a Ph.D at Claremont College, Ca. She has published in various church magazines and is the author of a book of poetry, *Line Upon Line* published by Bookcraft. Her husband is Sterling E. Ottesen and they are the parents of five. She has taught in seminary and institute programs of the church.

Marlene Jones Payne practices adult and child psychiatry in McLean, Virginia and teaches psychiatry at Georgetown University medical school. She is married to John Payne and they are the parents of two children. She enjoys training horses, and also designs and quilts wall hangings. Marlene's essay in this collection won Honorable Mention in the "Mormon Women Speak" contest.

Cherie Taylor Pedersen is a freelance writer from Mercersburg, Pa. She graduated from BYU with a BA in English. She is married to Carl D. Pedersen, is the mother of four children, and currently serves as Primary President of the York Pennsylvania Stake. She recently published in *Redbook Magazine.*

Dolores Chase Ritchie is currently working on a graduate degree in Arts Administration at the University of Utah. She formerly taught for the Humanities Department at BYU. She has two children, Marcelyn 21, a senior at the University of Utah and Marc, age 16.

Karen Rosenbaum is associate professor of English at Ohlone Junior College in Fremont, Ca. where she has been teaching since 1967. She has published short fiction in *Dialogue, Sunstone, Exponent II* and has been anthologized in several collections. A graduate of the Wallace Stegner creative writing program at Stanford, she is the winner of the Association of Mormon Letters award for fiction and Honorable Mention in the "Mormon Women Speak" contest.

RevaBeth Loveridge Russell is married to W. Keith Russell. They recently moved to Springville, Utah, with their three children. She received her BA Degree from BYU in biological science. Presently she is teaching part-time at Lehi High School and at Mountain View Hospital in Payson. RevaBeth writes that while she has published in the *Ensign, Exponent II,* and *Mother's Manual,* most of her literary endeavors consist of grocery lists and notes to her children's teachers.

Dian Saderup will graduate from the BYU with a degree in English. She has published fiction and articles in *The New Era, The Friend, Dialogue, Sunstone, BYU Studies, Exponent II* and *Century II.* She is currently collaborating with a psychologist on a novel for children.

Donna Toland Smart graduated from the University of Wyoming and received her MA Degree from the University of Utah. She has taught high school in Star Valley, Wyoming and at East High in Salt Lake. She has published in the *Relief Society Magazine, Ensign,* and *The Friend.* She and her husband, William B. Smart, are the parents of five word oriented children who love reading and writing. She enjoys golf, tennis, and backpacking.

Helen Candland Stark received her BA from BYU in 1924. She taught in Bingham, Jordan, Kanab and Brandywine high schools in Utah before returning to BYU for a Master's Degree. She won two Relief Society Magazine poetry contests and has published essays in *Exponent II* and *Sunstone.* She is one of the founders of the Alice Reynolds Club in Provo and serves on the boards of the BYU Women's Archives and the Utah Women's History Association. She and her husband, Henry, live in Salem, Utah, and are the parents of three.

Loretta Randall Sharp is on the writing faculty at the Interlochen Arts Academy, Interlochen, Michigan. She was valedictorian of her BYU graduating class and did her post graduate work at BYU. She was chosen Outstanding Young Woman of America. While at Interlochen she has administered a number of grants, one which established a fine arts major in writing at the Academy. She lectures on writing techniques at national organizations throughout the country.

Elizabeth Olson Wach recently retired as an English teacher, is a frequent contributor in children's fiction and humor, especially to the *Deseret News*. She reports that she has served in nearly all church capacities, including branch clerk and janitor. She does oil painting and is a member of the Schubert Singers in Salt Lake. She is married to Phillip H. Wach and they are the parents of four.

Marilyn Curtis White free-lance writer, was born in Washington, D.C. She received her BA from Brigham Young University in Journalism. She has served as a lobbyist at the Hawaii State Legislature and editor of *The Forum,* a newsletter for Hana Pono. Recently she was chosen to serve as resource chairman for the American Association of Women. Her husband Weston J. White is an attorney and they are the parents of eight children.